'A woman's preaching,' said Dr Johnson, 'is like a dog's walking on his hinder legs. It is not done well; but you are surprised to find it done at all.'

As a woman and staunch advocate of women's rights, a Congregational minister whose marriage to an Anglican priest was obstructed for years by the Church of England hierarchy, the Rev Elsie Chamberlain must have much occasion to reflect on the Doctor's dictum. But Elsie was born to show Dr Johnson just how wrong he could be!

Janette Williams's biography sheds a daughter's unique perspective on a brave and brilliant career. The former dress designer from Islington was the first woman chaplain in the Armed Forces; first ordained woman on the staff of BBC's Religious Broadcasting, and responsible for *Lift Up Your Hearts*, with its three million listeners; first woman chairman of the Congregational Union of England and Wales, and the first to present *The Daily Service* on BBC radio.

But if it is as a familiar and well-loved voice on the air that Elsie Chamberlain is best remembered, her daughter's book, written with a 'strong compulsion', shows us the person and the mind behind that voice. And the stuff of which history is made.

☆   ☆   ☆

The author, Janette Williams, daughter of Elsie Chamberlain, was urged to write this fascinating account by Elsie Chamberlain's friends.

Janette Williams is a teacher and lives in Gravesend.

First Lady of the Pulpit

A Biography of Elsie Chamberlain

Janette Williams

The Book Guild
Sussex, England

The Book Guild Ltd.
25 High Street,
Lewes, Sussex

First published 1993
© Janette Williams 1993

Set in Baskerville
Type setting by Kudos Graphics, Slinfold, West Sussex

Printed in Great Britain by
Antony Rowe Ltd.
Chippenham, Wiltshire

A catalogue record for this book is available
from the British Library

ISBN 0 86332 842 3

CONTENTS

LIST OF ILLUSTRATIONS

Centre section photographs:

Annie Chamberlain, Elsie's mother
James Chamberlain, Elsie's father
Elsie, aged six months
Brothers Ronald and Sidney hold their baby sister, 'Ithe Erl'
Elsie, Christmas 1912
Elsie's birthplace – 30 Canonbury Park North, Islington, London
Elsie, aged fifteen
A family group
The Chamberlain family – Ronald, Mother, Father, Elsie and Sidney
Islington Chapel where Elsie spent much of her spare time as a child
Having fun at the Islington Chapel
Miss E.D. Chamberlain (seen with her mother), 1939
King's College, Faculty of Theology, 1936–1937
Elsie's fiance, the Rev John Garrington, 1937
Squadron officer and chaplain Rev Elsie Chamberlain
Pre-wedding photo of the Rev John Garrington and the Rev Elsie
    Chamberlain
Newly-weds John and Elsie Garrington, with their best man
'Vicar marries woman chaplain', *The Advertiser*, Adelaide, 19th July
    1947
Newly ordained minister, Rev Elsie Chamberlain
The only surviving photograph of the Garrington family, 1956
John and Elsie
John (Garry) and myself
Elsie and I making curtains
John and Elsie shared a passion for sketching
Rev Elsie Chamberlain, 1956
Greensted Rectory was Elsie's favourite home
Elsie painting the window frame of 'Gable End'
Rev Elsie Chamberlain seated at her desk in her BBC office
Rev Elsie Chamberlain, producer of 'Lift up your hearts'
Elsie's father, Jim Chamberlain
Elsie's mother, Annie Chamberlain
The central service of the women's World Day of Prayer, 1962
John and Elsie at home in the lounge at Greensted Rectory
Foundation of the Congregational Federation ceremony
Rev Elsie Chamberlain, 1988
Elsie enjoyed a good joke
John Garrington
Rev Elsie Chamberlain

Dedicated in memory of two very dear people,

John and Elsie Garrington.

PREFACE

After my mother died in April 1991 I had the daunting task of clearing her Nottingham flat. Among masses of papers I found a buff folder containing her biographical notes. It was her intention to write her autobiography, when she had the time. Alas, it was one aim she didn't manage to achieve! As her only daughter, I have written her life story for her. I have made extensive use of her notes, personal letters, photographs, news cuttings and articles and her personal mementoes. I hope I have done justice to her and her work. My aim is to tell you who she was and what she did.

'Forceful, dynamic, caring, hater of humbug, simple, killjoy, fanatic, powerful ally, formidible enemy, redoubtable, controversial, genuine, sincere, gifted, marvellous, pioneer, adamant, charming,' have all been words to describe my mother, the Reverend Elsie Chamberlain. No doubt most are true! She was not flawless or without faults. She was a lady of high principles and strong religious convictions. Her views and thoughts allowed little room for compromise with others. She was adamant, if not obstinate, with little room for manoeuvre or negotiation. Yet this remarkable woman, with amazing energy and strength of character, won the respect and admiration of many associates. One can forgive her faults because she achieved so much good and was a true and faithful Christian all her life.

To be the first to do this or that was not Elsie's objective in life. To be a first class Christian and minister was her goal. She cared for others and sought to improve the quality of their lives by sharing her faith and experience. These are the aims she achieved. As her husband, John Garrington, said 'She is first rate in anything she does.'

9

1

Early Life

Elsie's parents were James and Annie Chamberlain. James Chamberlain was educated at the Dame Alice Owen School in Islington. When he left school he went to work in the General Post Office. He worked long, unsociable hours. He met and fell instantly in love with Annie Hayward, who was the middle daughter of a widow, Maria Hayward. She had been widowed at an early age and left with three young daughters to bring up. Annie was young and very pretty. She was clever and inclined to be self-willed – a fault she had been warned 'to guard against' at the age of fifteen! She had attended a Church of England school which was open to all ages. She started to train as a pupil teacher when she reached school leaving age. She found the work too tiring for her and so she gave it up and entered a City firm as a bookkeeper.

Annie was a strict teetotaller. She was told by her employer that when reps called in his absence she was to offer them a glass of sherry. She proffered it in such a voice and manner that they dared not say yes!

James (generally called Jim) Chamberlain was an ardent Anglican and a keen member of the Muswell Hill Parish Church choir. As a boy Jim had formed a friendship with the choirmaster who, finding the boy had a good soprano voice, trained and encouraged him. He became a boy soloist of some repute in the area around St Matthew's Church in City Road. It was this choirmaster that made it possible for Jim to go to the Dame Alice Owen School, where he was an exemplary pupil. His soprano voice later developed into a fine tenor so he performed as a chorister from the age of eight until he was eighty. As a young man Jim always wore for church a smart top hat which, on weekdays, he kept in a box under the bed. James was a mild-mannered gentleman who, early on in life, had been taught to say a definite 'please' and 'thank you'. One day as he was on his way to work, walking along the street, a pony and trap stopped. 'Would you like a lift, young sir?' enquired the driver. 'I don't mind if I do,' replied Jim, to which the driver retorted, 'and I don't mind if you don't,' and drove off leaving the surprised Jim to continue his way on foot!

James and Annie were married on 25 September 1897. Their first home was in Grange Road (later re-named Grange Grove), Islington, where they rented three upstairs rooms in a pleasant two-storey Victorian house. The first children born to the Chamberlains were twin sons. It was a difficult confinement but Annie refused to have a doctor in attendance or go into hospital. As a consequence one twin died at birth. The surviving child was called Sidney James. Two years later another son was born, named Ronald Arthur. In 1904 Mr and Mrs Chamberlain and their young family moved to 30 Canonbury Park North, in a middle class area of Islington. This was a large semi-detached house with three storeys. The Chamberlains occupied the two lower storeys whilst Annie's mother and two unmarried sisters lived on the upper floor. The family employed a maid to help with the chores. She lived in an attic room and was paid the princely sum of £5 per annum! The third addition to the family was a daughter, Irene, but she was a sickly child who had a skin complaint. The self-willed Annie had absolute faith in her doctor and, despite pleas from Jim for a second medical opinion, she remained obstinate. Irene died and Annie became ill because she was accused by a medical practitioner of poisoning her daughter by giving her tea! During this time Annie's mother, Maria Hayward, took charge of the household.

Six years after the death of Irene another daughter was

born, Elsie Dorothea. She was born in the family home on 3 March 1910. She was much loved by all the family. Her brothers adored her and were willing child minders. In a letter, dated 27 August 1912 written by Ronnie to his father, he states: "I'm helping mother a lot, three times I have got Elsie to sleep and I often mind and play with her too".

Elsie was the favoured child and the 'baby' of the family. Her mother doted on her and called her Dearie Pet. She was dressed like a doll – her grandmother had her bonnets, ribbons and bows meticulously ironed before wear. Elsie was always called Little Elsie, which the infant Elsie had a job to pronounce. She managed 'Ithe Erl' and 'Ithe Erl' became the family nickname. The 'Ithe' bit was dropped as she became older. Elsie was given a fear of illness – she was protected and sheltered from all ailments, however minor. When the two boys became ill Elsie was kept well apart from them. This happened when Ron contracted a very bad attack of chicken pox but Elsie caught it – she had one spot on one of her hands. She was very proud of that one spot!

Both Jim and Annie had strong religious convictions but the children of the marriage went to Annie's church, which was the Congregational Chapel in Islington. At that time, this chapel had a fashionable middle class congregation. Beneath the chapel was a hall where a special evening service was held for the underprivileged. These included the servants, who were not free to come to the morning service as they were busy at work in their employers' houses. Also it was suggested that they would feel ill at ease worshipping with the smarter folk upstairs!

Sunday was a day set aside for worship. Father would go to his church, the local Anglican one, whilst Mother and children attended the Congregational Chapel in Islington. The family would meet for lunch, which had been previously prepared by the maid. Then, over lunch, they would discuss their services and sermons. In the afternoon the children would go to Sunday school. Afterwards they would come home for a special tea with cake and then go to the adult evening service with Mother. On one occasion when

Annie was out shopping, she met the local vicar. He knew her to be the wife of one of his regular parishioners but he wondered why she didn't come to his church. She replied 'I send my husband every week. I can only spare him for you. I go elsewhere.'

Breakfast was a family meal and Annie read aloud from the Bible while the family ate. They listened to the selected reading whilst Mother's breakfast was perched over a cup of hot liquid to keep it warm. The family always had a cooked breakfast and Elsie said in later life, 'I was more interested in my lovely cooked breakfast than the Bible reading!'

The family had at least one annual holiday together, usually at the seaside. Their favourite places were East-bourne and Chideock in Dorset. Jim was a keen cyclist and walker. Annie and Elsie did not like these pursuits but the two boys would make short trips with Father. On their annual holiday Annie and the children would go together and Father would cycle. They would meet at their chosen destination. Sometimes Jim would cycle to the holiday spot and fix up the accommodation and then the family would follow. This happened in August 1912, because Ronnie wrote to his father thanking him for the 'views of Budleigh Salterton'. He goes on to say, 'It seems a very nice place, and as it is a small place, it will not be far from the sea and not a long drag up the cliff like at Pokesdown. There are some nice houses on the sea front, if we could get an apartment in one of those. I hope you are having a nice trip on your "bisicley".'

Annie Chamberlain didn't like housework or cooking. A maid was employed to keep the house clean, whilst her mother did the washing, ironing and cooking. Years later, Annie used to say, with great pride, 'I never had to do housework.' Her job was to supervise the chores, the shopping and the menus. She used to enjoy the shopping but housework was definitely not for her! She also was the children's educator and insisted on organising the spare time for each child. They were encouraged to paint and draw and she taught them all to read and write. Ron, the younger son, was a talented pianist, so music was fostered. Sidney was the least musical of the three but he was the artist in the family. Elsie learnt to play the violin and was encouraged to sing. Sidney was expected to do well for himself and for his dead twin. Likewise, Elsie had to do well for herself and for her late sister. During the First World War Sidney joined the newly formed Flying Corps, an act of which his mother didn't approve. The family, like others in these war years, was affected by shortages. It was a big shock to Annie when she thought she was queueing for bread to find that the queue was for the cinema! After that 'dreadful' experience, Annie made her sisters or the maid do the queueing!

Elsie started school during the war years. She followed her brothers who had previously attended the Dame Alice Owen School. Jim Chamberlain was an old boy. Elsie said in later life, 'My parents gave up luxuries so that their children could have the best education they could afford'.

The Dame Alice Owen School had been founded in 1613 for the education of working class children. There was a separate school for boys and girls. The school governors were the Worshipful Company of Brewers, so it is clear that Annie had to let tradition override her principles about alcohol on this occasion! However, the girls' school motto, 'Instead of being made − make yourself' no doubt appealed to Annie. Elsie's school report for the year 1919 shows that she was 'good' or 'very good' in all listed subjects save arithmetic, geometry and singing! Her behaviour was credited as 'good but talkative'. This school gave Elsie a strong academic background. She left there at the age of ten to become a pupil at Channing School for Girls in Highgate.

Channing School for Girls was founded in 1885 by the Rev. Robert Spears and two sisters, Mathilda and Emily Sharpe. It had been named in honour of William Ellery Channing, an eminent American philosopher, Unitarian preacher, educationalist and author. It was described as a 'middle class, high school'. It was to provide a first class

Unitarian education for 'young ladies'. It was fee paying, so in some ways it was elitist. The school was mainly for boarders but Elsie entered as a day girl. A school uniform was compulsory. The girls wore navy blue tunics, long-sleeved white blouses and thick black stockings. These stockings were worn throughout the year but, during the summer term, they could be removed once inside school and put on again at going home time. In the winter the girls wore navy blue felt hats, replaced in the summer by panamas. Like the black stockings, these had to be worn at all times outside the school gate. For special occasions a green dress was worn. The school provided Elsie with a first class education; she was very proud to be a Channing girl. In later life, if she was in the neighbourhood, she would make a detour, 'just to look at the place'. Miss Haigh was the headmistress for most of Elsie's time there. Elsie used to refer to her as 'a dragon' – a dragon who was very insistent on 'the correct decorum as befits young ladies'. You obeyed the rules and regulations or suffered the consequences, which was often a very lengthy lecture. She would walk down the corridor with a stick in hand and when you saw her you tried to look 'small, sweet and angelic'. Nonetheless, Elsie had a high regard for the formidable Miss Haigh.

Miss Haigh held divinity classes in her room. The girls sat on the floor. The lesson was more about moral issues than religious instruction. Personal and social behaviour, citizenship, how best to use leisure time, and literary topics were discussed in 'an adult way with an adult'.

Day girls had their lunch at school. Talking at the meal table was permitted. Eight girls sat at each table with a member of staff at one end. The seating at the table was changed daily so that each girl had the opportunity to sit next to the teacher and converse with her. In the school magazines that Elsie saved are many entries of her achievements – form captain, vice captain for netball and games, hockey captain and prefect. In the year 1924 to 1925 she was the recipient of a scholarship worth £10 per annum.

16

This was probably enough to pay for one year's school fees in those days! Her academic achievements are also well documented. She gained certificates for her violin playing, singing, diction and elocution, medals and certificates for poetry reading and for matriculation. Miss Haigh always encouraged each pupil to do her best.

Elsie's great passion at school was not divinity or music but games. She loved hockey and at one time even considered becoming a games teacher. She wrote, 'I narrowly missed becoming a games mistress. In my last term at school, I deputised as the games mistress but I found it all too frustrating to little girls, who were being coerced to 'run' or 'hit it' or 'catch it' when the last thing they wanted to do was any of those things!'

Outside school hours time was spent doing homework, practising on her violin and going to Islington Chapel, where she would help her mother by serving teas, talking to the lonely and minding the younger children. Her two elder brothers married when she was in her teens. She became an aunt to two nephews and one niece; she would mind them and take them out for the occasional treat. She enjoyed being an aunt. Elsie's life was centred around her family and Islington Chapel. The house in Canonbury Park North, which Jim and Annie bought in 1904, was in need of major repair. The family moved to another part of North London, Muswell Hill.

Elsie left school in 1927, undecided about her goal in life. The only sure thing was that she didn't want to be a games mistress! She continued her music studies and gained a teaching diploma, enabling her to teach the violin. She also gained an elocution diploma. Elsie thought about becoming a professional violinist but she felt she didn't have the 'nerve and calmness' required for a performer and for teaching the violin day in and day out. 'Listening to those awful scratchy noises children make when they're trying to learn is unbearable!' she said. She soon realized that a career as a teacher of the violin was not for her!

Elsie started a part-time course at an art college, studying

17

dress design. She found she had a flair for design so she took a job in an East End clothing factory as a very junior assistant in the design office. She didn't remain a junior assistant for long since the senior designer left 'in a huff', making that post vacant. At this time, Elsie still lived with her parents and led a very sheltered existence. She was discouraged from wearing make-up and had no boy friends.

Jim Chamberlain retired in 1933. He had spent all his working life employed by the GPO and when he left he was presented with an award for long faithful service by the King. He had a special wish to visit South Africa. Both Annie and Elsie were asked to accompany him on the trip but Annie didn't want to go, so she and Elsie stayed in England and Jim brought them a car instead! Elsie's brothers taught her to drive and Elsie never took a driving test in her whole life, since in those days formal driving tests were not compulsory. Elsie's grandmother, Maria Hayward, died at the grand age of ninety nine and one of Annie's unmarried sisters also died at about the same time.

Meanwhile more and more of Elsie's spare time was spent at the Chapel. Elsie said, 'Occasionally I'd realize that I was spending most of my free time in a place where there were few people of my own age and interest – I'd feel like breaking out and having fun . . .' Then she realized that she was having fun and the minister, the Rev Robert Shepherd, suggested that maybe church work was her vocation.

Elsie mixed well with people and enjoyed their company. She was drawn more and more into the church, encouraged by her minister. She wanted to learn Hebrew so the Rev Shepherd ran Hebrew classes for those interested. The church and involvement in it became a regular night-time job and gradually Elsie began to tire of her daytime work. She realized that she couldn't face another cut-out dress. 'I loved designing them, but wasn't so keen on making them up.' She knew she couldn't spend the rest of her life sketching, so she gave up her lucrative job. Her father didn't like the idea of her relinquishing a well-paid position, particularly when it was to train for a vocation which, in all probability, she might never have the opportunity of filling. But her parents were very understanding about it so the decision was made. Elsie wanted to train for the ministry. She gave up her daytime job and started freelance designing to earn enough money to see her through university. When Elsie decided that she wished to enter the ministry she approached a college professor who said to her that even if she were trained there was no guarantee that a church would call her to be its minister. Her answer was prompt and to the point 'If that happens then I'll go back to dress designing.'

She knew then that it would be an uphill struggle as she was a woman about to trespass in what was, and is still, very much a man's world.

2

Reverend Elsie Chamberlain

King's College, London had, in those days, a theological faculty, used by the Church of England as a place of training for ordinands, but still available to any matriculated students to study for a Bachelor of Divinity degree. Elsie had discovered that the Congregational theological colleges were still not willing to train women. The principal of New College at that time explained carefully that when his students needed a reprimand, he rebuked them in his study, which he found difficult with women. Elsie always wished she had asked him why. He was thoroughly Victorian! Elsie went to see Dr Nathaniel Miklem at Mansfield College, Oxford, who was quite willing to have her for two year's pastoral and Congregational training after she had graduated. So, somewhat encouraged, she settled in at King's College among well over 200 Anglican students (including the women who were doing the Lambeth diploma). Only two other women were on the degree course, one a Methodist and the other an Anglican. Elsie was not upset by the phalanx of Anglicans at King's – though somewhat concerned by what she considered to be ignorance and narrow-mindedness about other branches of the Christian Church. Being challenged sometimes about her Congregationalism only made her a better Congregationalist with clear reasons for her faith, as well as broadening her understanding of the Church of England and the gulf that sometimes appeared between the 'spikes', the Evangelists, the high and the low.

John Garrington, a fellow student, was on the high side. He had been educated in a Roman Catholic seminary, with the priesthood in view. At seventeen, he left school and worked for a while in his father's tailoring business in Aberystwyth. He then went on to do some journalism and at the same time acquired an interest in psychology. But he had known his vocation to the priesthood since the age of seven and entered King's College as an ordinand with the backing of his local bishop. He was president of the theological faculty and was in his second year when Elsie enrolled as a student. Elsie represented the women students, who were, of course in the minority.

It was the president's job to keep the other students informed of forthcoming events, lectures, and so on. He would put up the notices for the male students and Elsie would put them up for the female students; the trouble was the women had no right to have such information and so they were removed from the notice board by the male president! This act did not please Elsie. How dare that arrogant male president remove her notices? She went in search of him. The notice board in the East Corridor could hardly be called a romantic place to meet one's future husband but that is where John and Elsie first met! Their first meeting was purely on business matters. Elsie wanted, or demanded, that the women should have part of the notice board. Very grudgingly, a portion of the board was given to them.

One day Elsie heard that John Garrington wished to see her. 'Who's he?' she asked, and when informed he was the 'arrogant' male president, she went in search of him. From this meeting Elsie gathered, to her delight, that the men wanted closer cooperation with the female students. A little more conversation revealed that the men's society was 'broke'. The women were few but had somehow accumulated a bank balance. So it became obvious that the desire for closer cooperation was for the sole purpose of amalgamating funds. Elsie wrote, 'I was not flattered and Garrington realized that Chamberlain was not as simple as she

21

looked!' However, the interest in each other increased and by the time Elsie had completed her degree she was engaged to 'that arrogant John Garrington.'

After his finals John was ordained in St Paul's Cathedral and attached as deacon to St Martin's Church, Kensal Rise. He always said he got that job because the vicar there discovered he could read Dante in the original text! The romance continued to flourish. John believed in Elsie's sense of vocation, as she believed in his.

Before completing her finals, Elsie attended Annadale for an inter-theological conference and she heard the Rev Muriel Paulden give a stirring lecture. The Rev Muriel Paulden had been trained for the mission field at Selly Oak. She had already bought her ticket for India when it was discovered that she had double curvature of the spine and the London Missionary Society would not allow her to go and work in under developed countries. Her motto in life was to be ready for anything. As she couldn't be a missionary she started a training centre at Berkley Street in Liverpool. The centre was for the training of Sunday school and day school teachers. There were people in most of the Merseyside Free Churches who attended Miss Paulden's lectures. She made the Bible especially exciting and had a great following. She gave two lectures of one hour duration most evenings. At first ministers had been loathe to let their members join the training centre, thinking that they might be drawn into Miss Paulden's church in Berkley Street – but this was not the objective and the objectors soon found they had more able and useful church members as a result of the course.

Elsie heard that Muriel was looking for an assistant minister for her church in a poor area of Liverpool. Elsie asked if she would be suitable. Muriel visited Elsie in the family home in Muswell Hill and arranged for her to go and preach in the Liverpool church. After this Elsie received an official invitation to be an assistant minister. Dr Sidney Berry, secretary of the Congregational Union of England and Wales, then had to be consulted. What about the projected two years at Mansfield? Would the Ministerial Training Committee accept the work in Liverpool as part of Elsie's equipment for ordination? To Elsie's relief it was decided that work with the Rev Muriel Paulden would be an excellent opportunity to complete her training.

So, at the beginning of August 1939, Elsie's elder brother, Sidney, drove her to Berkley street with a carload of effects. It was a hot day. Her study was situated in the basement of the church and it smelt warm, damp and mousy. The damp was caused by the fact that the floor of the schoolroom, off which her study opened, was mopped every day with disinfectant – for the benefit of a flourishing nursery school she was to run. The smell of mice remained because the place was overrun with the little creatures. Elsie could remember working on many sermons, sitting on the table because the mice were scuttling around! Elsie wrote, 'This went on, until in the Lord's good time, he sent a stray kitten into her midst. Jose (that did for Joseph or Josephine) was all eyes and skinny and her presence provided a grand deterrent to the mice. She seemed to be a religious cat, insisting on coming to church on auspicious and inauspicious occasions!' Before Jose and Elsie had time to settle in, war with Germany was declared. Immediately the whole scheme of work changed. Elsie found lodgings in a local hostel and phoned her parents to inform them of her new abode. Annie Chamberlain was far from pleased to hear that her Elsie was living in a hostel. In a letter to Elsie, she wrote, 'I think you would like a home better than a hostel.' Despite the war, Annie and Jim Chamberlain made the decision to move to Liverpool.

Jim wrote 'We don't like being separated by such a long distance but we're hoping to be nearer soon.'

In a letter dated 7 September 1939, Annie wrote to Elsie, '. . . we shall certainly want to find a house, as we do not know how long the war may go on. I still hope that it will not be long and Daddy and Sidney both think it will not, but anyway we should find it fairly easy to find somewhere as lots of people will have moved out of Liverpool.'

Elsie's parents did move to Liverpool and she shared their flat with them.

After war was declared Muriel Paulden, nicknamed Paul, had arranged to borrow a nearby YMCA hut to serve refreshments to the troops, who were living in a transit camp on the opposite side of the road. They also converted the schoolroom of the church for billiards, table tennis and letter writing.This completely changed the programme of church activities. As the blackout made crossing the Mersey a hazard at night, so the attendance at the training centre for teachers dwindled overnight. The Liverpool blackout was so complete that at first vehicles had no lights at all. The clanky old trams could be heard coming – but not seen. Crossing the Mersey by boat was not encouraged after dark and when the bombing began the Mersey tunnel became a dormitory for masses of people who had no other safe shelter. Then there was the great evacuation programme. Most of the Sunday school children went off to homes in the country. Paul and Elsie visited them to see that they had settled down. Before long nearly all the children were back home again because bombing had not begun. The children missed the chip shops and the pictures – they were not trained for country life.

One evening, Elsie came out of a house which she had visited and impaled herself on some low railings in the pitch darkness. A couple came to her rescue and as she staggered home any passerby might well have thought she had shared a party at one of the locals!

The Blitz began the following year and Liverpool suffered badly. The 'all clear' often went in the early hours when Elsie was going home. Then Elsie cycled home between the tramlines. Her annual salary of £150 permitted the purchase of a bicycle but not a car; cars were in big demand to help with the war effort. Paul had an ancient car which was used to transport evacuees, the sick and the elderly.

One Sunday, after a baptism, Elsie drove the baby and its grandmother back to Bootle in Paul's ancient car. There had been a bad raid in the night and Bootle, which was near the docks, had taken the force. Elsie said that it was the nearest to Hell she ever wanted to be. After a night of blitz there were still fires burning and the remains of buildings collapsing into streets, and this meant making long detours to avoid the hazards. There was dereliction everywhere. The canteen opposite the barracks was in great demand. Also the church hall, providing amenities for games, letter writing, a place to meet, relax and chat. Elsie could recall a great big Scot coming into the canteen with a shilling to buy a cup of tea and eleven cakes – they still made a profit! Elsie's work during this time in Liverpool was to 'lend an ear' to soldiers, particularly the very young soldiers and to those suffering the death of a loved one. She became a very good listener.

Meanwhile, John was having a worse time in London, with almost nightly bombing. Once when Elsie was phoning from Liverpool, John said, 'hold on! there's one coming, I'll lie down.' She heard the crump over the phone and said goodbye rather hurriedly. At that time John was curate of St Mary Abbot, Kensington High Street and also a part-time air raid warden. He helped to extinguish fires and free those trapped in the bomb debris. The romance between him and Elsie was beginning to meet with difficulties. Annie was against the union. She often forgot to pass on messages. In September 1940 John wrote a letter to Elsie and he ends, 'Course, I might be able to come and see you but I don't want to complicate things with your folks. Can I phone you?' and again in another letter, dated December 1940, John wrote, 'Happy New Year! I hope all will go well with us in 1941.'

But Elsie was under tremendous pressure from her mother and her engagement with John was broken off.

Elsie experienced some of the horrors of war during her time in Liverpool. She was there during bombing raids and met very young soldiers, among whom were some who did not return. She became involved with the emotional problems of those who lost husbands, boyfriends, sons and brothers. She helped those who were made homeless and

25

those who were wounded and bereaved. As a result of these experiences Elsie became a lifelong advocate for peace.

In 1941, at the end of her 'apprenticeship', Elsie was received into the Roll of Congregational Ministers. She was now the Rev Elsie Chamberlain.

3

First Lady Chaplain

The Rev Elsie Chamberlain's next move in the Congregational ministry was a call to Christ Church in Friern Barnet, a church situated opposite one of London's largest lunatic asylums. Elsie wondered if that had any connection with the calling for a woman minister! She was glad to be back in familiar surroundings. Her parents, who had shared a large flat in Liverpool, bought a house in Friern Barnet, and Elsie and her parents moved back to London, although the 1939–1945 war was still waging. After a time the bombing was replaced by attack by V1 rocket (the 'Doodlebugs'). They were unnerving because you could hear them coming; there was time to decide what action to take.

Elsie remembered being in the Middlesex Guildhall, in Westminster, pleading for special treatment for a boy she considered deserving and clever but who had failed his eleven-plus because he was nervous. The siren went and a polite official offered her the shelter of a cupboard on the third floor. This offered little protection against a direct hit but some safety against flying glass. The thing passed over and the boy got his place and the last Elsie heard of him was that he was a solicitor in South Africa.

Elsie worked tirelessly with the children in her church. She was much concerned about the psychological damage caused by the ravages of war. The children were, on the whole, without their fathers, who had been drafted into the Armed Forces. She ran clubs especially aimed at children – she had a tot-teens club, a youth club and an orchestra. She began to teach the violin again. Pupils were charged 6d. for a lesson, lasting a quarter of an hour. This fee went to the Bombed Churches fund. She ran a 'cleaning up' brigade and a canteen for soldiers on leave, soldiers' wives and the elderly. People would come to the church, asking to see the minister. They were often directed to someone with soapy water dripping from elbows and wisps of hair hanging down! She also helped and cheered the sick and wounded from Friern Hospital.

From her pulpit Elsie gained a reputation for plain outspoken speech. She was an ardent teetotaler and she took steps to hold up free beer, provided by the Red Cross, for repatriated soldiers. Elsie was accused of being a killjoy and a fanatic. She threatened to withhold her own subscription from the Red Cross. Elsie was quite unrepentent: she said: 'I am staunch teetotaller and so are many of my congregation. I have to stand up for my principles. It is not easy to do these unpopular things.'

This pronouncement caused a big stir and it became headline news in many of the national newspapers. There were letters of support, some from those who were outraged and disgusted. Eventually a footnote appeared in the *Daily Express* dated 30 November 1943 which simply read 'The Red Cross and St John War Organisation which received a "few dozen" letters protesting about beer being supplied to repatriated prisoners want the whole thing to be forgotten. But haven't those 'few dozen' people left a nasty taste?'

Elsie was invited to speak at Speakers Corner in Hyde Park. Here she gained invaluable experience in dealing with large gatherings as the article on page 29 illustrates.

It was while Elsie was minister at Christ Church that she received an invitation to become a chaplain in the Royal Air Force.

At King's College, Elsie had formed a firm friendship with Margaret Stansgate, a lady who today would be called a 'mature student'. She was studying Hebrew and the mother of three sons. Her husband, William, was a politician. After the Conservatives lost the 1945 election Clement Atlee became the new prime minister. He invited Lord Stansgate to join the Cabinet as Secretary of State for Air. Before he left for Downing Street, Margaret Stansgate said to her husband, 'If you are offered the Air Ministry, you will make Elsie Chamberlain a chaplain in the RAF, won't you?'

Lord Stansgate was tremendously keen to have a lady chaplain in the Air Force and Elsie was the chaplain he planned to have! Elsie's name was put before the United Board of Chaplains with strong support from the Secretary of State for Air, Lord Stansgate. She was offered the chaplaincy. Lord Stansgate sent a message in advance to King George VI and the Queen about the appointment of the first woman chaplain to the Forces and was told that Their Majesties thought it was a good move! However, the appointment was not well received by the Church of England dignitaries. There was considerable scheming and unbelievable objections to the idea and great machinations went on to prevent the Air Minister from going ahead with the appointment of a Free Church woman chaplain. Lord

Stansgate received this letter from the Archbishop of Canterbury about the proposed appointment:

Lambeth Palace, S.E.1

20th March, 1946

My Dear Lord Stansgate,
'The Times' to-day announces the appointment as an R.A.F. Chaplain of the Rev. Elsie Chamberlain. I cannot but deeply regret that you have not heeded my warning that this would cause confusion and trouble. It appears that in fact her commission is as a Squadron Officer in the W.A.A.F. To that of course there is no objection, but her description as a Chaplain will certainly bring me enquiries to which I shall have to be able to give a clear answer. May I therefore put the following questions:

1. Is Squadron Officer Chamberlain in fact also a member of the Chaplains' Department of the R.A.F.?
2. In that case is she as such under the orders of the Chaplain-in-Chief and are her activities as a Chaplain controlled by him? If not, who does control her activities as a Chaplain?
3. In any case may I have an assurance that as a Chaplain she will not be permitted to exercise her ministry or take Services for Church of England personnel? In particular, under what conditions, if any, will she be allowed to administer the Sacraments of the Congregational Church and what steps will be taken to secure that all Church of England personnel are strictly warned that under no conditions must they either intentionally or by inadvertence attend Services at which she administers

the sacraments.

I am sorry that the position has arisen in which I am compelled to put these questions. They need never have arisen if the admirable example of the Army had been followed and she had been appointed as a Chaplain's Assistant.

4. May I also be assured that in no circumstances will any Church of England Chaplain be put into the position of accepting orders about Services or their conduct from her or of being associated with her in their conduct?

Yours sincerely

GEOFFREY CANTUAR

The Rt. Hon. The Viscount Stansgate,
Secretary of State of Air,
Air Ministry,
Whitehall, S.W.1.

The appointment was eventually made. However, when the RAF list was published Elsie's name was listed in the welfare section and Lord Stansgate was far from pleased! He had the original lists pulped and a new document printed in which Elsie's name was included amongst the chaplains.

In March 1946, Elsie took up her appointment. She held the rank of a squadron officer in the WAAF but at the same time, a chaplaincy in the RAF. She wore the squadron officer's uniform and the chaplain's insignia and stole, but not a clerical collar. Elsie and Lady Stansgate went to Wippell's, the clerical tailors next to Westminster Abbey, to buy the stole. The assistant assumed that Elsie was buying it for her husband and when asked how tall he was, Elsie replied, 'About my height' and burst out laughing, which puzzled everyone in the shop!

31

WOMEN'S AUXILIARY AIR FORCE (W.A.A.F. "G" Branch)

7924	7925–99	8000–29
Section Officers	**1945**	**Woman Chaplain**
1943—contd.	Hutt, C. A. (w) 5Jan	**Squadron Officer**
Haselden, O. D. (w) 25May	Bridger, T. A. (w) 26Jan	
Pierce, D. M. (w) 25May	Essex, S. J. (w) 26Jan	*United Board—Rev.* Elsie
Pool, W. (w) 27May	Gardiner, B. T. (w) 26Jan	D. Chamberlain, B.D. Mar.46
	Granger, M. H. 26Jan	
Gilkes, K. F. (w) 7June	Hillman, M. F. (w) 26Jan	
MacKay, J. V. M. (w) 7June	Hucker, B. J. (w) 26Jan	
Sutton, M. A. (w) 9June	Macphail, J. (w) 26Jan	
Sanger-Davies, M. (w) 16June	Pawson, H. J. ( ) 26Jan	
Frampton, F. V. P. (w) 17June	Plant, I. E. (w) 26Jan	
West, M. (w) 30June	Quickenden, M. St. C. (w) 26Jan	
Cole, M. C. (w) 1July	Ray, L. C. C. (w) 26Jan	
Holdsworth, J. (w) 7July	Stephens, J. D. (w) 26Jan	
Anthony, C. M. T. (w) 27July	Simms, M. (w) 23Feb	
Johnston, K. (w) 27July	Morris, K. (w) 23Feb	
Sandys, H. M. (w) 27July	Metcalf, M. (w) 4Apr	
Scott, D. J. (w) 11Aug	Lewis, C. M. (w) 12May	
Baker, E. M. (w) 24Aug	Williams, E. B. (w) 27June	
Deverell, M. K. (w) 24Aug	Harland, M. M. (w) 2Nov	
Gadsdon, P. A. (w) 24Aug		
Greene, D. M. (w) 24Aug	**Assistant**	
Harboord, M. L. (w) 24Aug	**Section Officers**	
Peckham, W. M. (w) 24Aug	**1945**	
Mantell, E. C. C. (w) 8Sept	Wallbridge, D. 27June	
Clarke, B. W. (w) 14Oct	Barlow, W. H. 11July	
Aulton, H. N. (w) 24Oct	Goodman, K. M. 11July	
Steele, D. M. (w) 7Dec	Jackson, D. L. 11July	
	Michell, H. R. 11July	
	Benedek, M. V. 8Aug	
1944	Bennion, M. 8Aug	
	Carr, B. R. 8Aug	
Bashford, J. I. (w) 1Jan	Forbes, P. K. 8Aug	
McIntyre, J. McD (w) 14Jan	Ford, G. E. 8Aug	
McGiffin, J. M. (w) 11Feb	Gaddes, J. 8Aug	
Kingham, D. I. (w) 27Apr	Howard, G. R. 8Aug	
Miller, N (w) 26July	Morris, E. 8Aug	
Cowley, N. L. M. (w) 2Aug	Porchetta, P. I. 8Aug	
Pentney, E. N. (w) 2Aug	Rowe, B. A. 8Aug	
Franks, J. E. D. (w) 22Sept	Boyce, J. S. 22Aug	
	Donnelly, H. J. 30Oct	
	Gentry, C. M. 30Oct	
	Ivor-Evans, M. L. E. 30Oct	
	Johnston, B. M. 30Oct	
	Langley, J. D. E. 30Oct	
	McCall-Smith, A. B. 30Oct	
	Parsons, P. M. 30Oct	
	Pibworth, I. A. 30Oct	
	Redler, N. B. 30Oct	
	Reed, E. L 30Oct	
	Turnbull, D. J. 30Oct	

1025

RAF appointment's list with Elsie's name as chaplain. The first printed list was pulped on the orders of Lord Stansgate because Elsie's name appeared in the Welfare section.

Lord Stansgate wrote a letter to Elsie when she took up her appointment:'My dear Chaplain, I am very proud of the job. I hope all goes well with your pioneer work. It's about the only important thing that's happened for a long time.'

Elsie was installed at Cranwell, home of the RAF staff College, some fifteen miles from Lincoln. Some of the men were, to say the least, shocked when they came into the chaplain's office to be confronted with a lady chaplain! They considered calling her 'madre' instead of 'padre' but the men did accept her as a padre!

She acted as a padre to both men and women and most preferred talking to her rather than a man. The women more readily confided their intimate problems. She had an advantage over the male padres in that she could 'come and go' into the female quarters.

One of Elsie's most terrifying experiences was having to lead parade ground prayers for a couple of thousand men. She said, 'I knew I had really been accepted after my first parade ground prayers. Some of the men told me that they had heard me in the rear ranks and that had never happened before.'

From Cranwell Elsie was assigned to the RAF base at St Athan in Wales. There tragedy struck. Elsie found the climate wet and damp. These had an adverse effect on her health. She was struck down with 'infective arthritis'. She spent days in bed, unable to walk, and was eventually admitted into the local military hospital for further treatment. Her illness was a terrible shock. Lord Stansgate wrote a letter, dated 19 July 1946, saying 'I do hope you are on the mend. We have been much concerned . . . Do get better soon.'

The men's secretary of the Officers' Mess, J.G.S. Webb, wrote to suggest Doctor Bengue's Balsam as beneficial. Dr Sidney Berry, chairman of the Congregational Union of England and Wales wrote, 'I hope that this wretched trouble will soon be over.' But the ailment didn't improve and it was decided that a change in surroundings might be better for her. In November 1946 the Under Secretary of

AIR MINISTRY,

KING CHARLES STREET.

WHITEHALL, S.W.1.

16 November, 1946.

Dear *Ronald*

I write to let you know, as I think very probably you already do, that your sister, Chaplain Elsie Chamberlain, has now left St.Athans Hospital and is going to have private treatment at home for six weeks or so.

I hear from Sir John Conybeare, who visited your sister last Saturday, that she has been progressing towards recovery steadily though slowly over the last three months and he has every hope that it will be quite possible for her to take up her duties again in another three months time.   He quite agrees with her own feeling that a change of surroundings and atmosphere will be beneficial and has recommended that she has six weeks at home before having another Medical Board.

As a matter of fact, I gather our medical authorities at St.Athan had intended to allow your sister to go home, but kept her in hospital a short while longer than they intended, when they heard that Sir Conybeare was visiting her.   I hope now she will make full progress towards recovery.

Yours sincerely,

Geoffrey de Freitas.

R.A.Chamberlain, Esq., M.P.,
House of Commons,
S.W.1.

State for Air, Geoffrey de Freitas, wrote to Elsie's younger brother, who was now a MP.

Elsie came back to Friern Barnet. She received this letter from Dr Sidney Berry.

'There is certain to be another big job for you.' – This must have given Elsie, as an invalid, something to think about! After all, being a female in such a male dominated area was a tremendous feat and privilege.

THE CONGREGATIONAL UNION
OF ENGLAND & WALES

Secretary: Rev. S.M.BERRY, M.A.,D.D.
Assistant : Rev. PHILIP ASHTON, B.A.
TEL. CENTRAL 1819
Finance: Mr. HAROLD SIMPSON, A.S.A.A.
TEL. CENTRAL 3936
TELEGRAMS: MEMORIAL, CENT, LONDON.

17th December 1946

MEMORIAL HALL
FARRINGDON ST.
LONDON E.C.4

My dear Elsie,

      I am awfully glad you have written to me. I have been wondering about you a lot, and I am thankful to hear you are home again now and out of the hands of R.A.F. medical orderlies and all that sort of business. It must be a perfect relief. But you are obviously a bit of a crock yet, and you will have to take very great care.

      I really don't anticipate you will get through that medical. In a way I shall be rather sorry if you do, because I don't think you ought to go back to the R.A.F. I think you might so easily get a recurrence of the trouble, and it might permanently damage your health. There is certain to be another big job for you. I have no doubt in my own mind about that, and you have established the principle which Lord Stansgate was determined to carry through; but it is no good you staying on in the R.A.F. if it is going to injure your health. Let me know immediately the result of the medical board is out, and then we will have to get to work on something else.

      I hope you will be able to contact the Stansgates. I have not seen them at all since I came back from America in the summer, but Lord Stansgate has been pretty well occupied with Egypt and has not had much chance, I am sure, to give to home affairs.

      Well, take care of yourself, and keep as patient as you can, and the way to the future will open. Meanwhile, the happiest possible Christmas to you.

            With all affectionate greetings,

                  Yours ever,

                     Sidney

Rev. Elsie Chamberlain.

Elsie's mother had read about a Swiss doctor who specialized in arthritic patients and who had devised a special diet for the sufferers of this condition. The diet involved drinking vast quantities of freshly squeezed lemon juice. Elsie had to drink undiluted lemon juice before partaking of any other drink or food. The number of squeezed lemons was gradually increased until she was drinking the juice of eighteen lemons in one glass!

The lemons were virtually unobtainable during the post war years. Elsie was forntunate to have a friend who worked for an airline and was able to get them for her from abroad. Gradually this lemon cure brought about an improvement to Elsie's condition. She was no longer bedridden but was still unable to resume her RAF duties. She failed her medical examination and so was invalided out of the Air Force. The complaint continued to affect Elsie until 1951. Up till then, she had to appear regularly before the Forces' medical Board and was receiving a disability pension until June 1951.

Despite her illness and short appointment, Elsie was very proud of her position as first woman chaplain in the Forces. Until her death, in 1991, she often wore her RAF stole at very special services and occasions.

4

Mrs Garrington

John and Elsie had planned to marry sometime in 1939, when Elsie had obtained her degree. Had their wedding taken place at this time they would not have encountered the many difficulties they faced later. The wedding was postponed because John fell seriously ill with scarlet fever at the outbreak of the 1939 war. He was confined to an isolation unit, and it was because of this illness that John was exempted from active war service. Elsie completed her degree course and was still Miss Elsie Chamberlain. She was set on becoming a minister and so she took up further training, which she completed in 1941. Now she became Reverend Elsie Chamberlain. The 'Reverend' was the crucial point. Elsie became well known as Elsie Chamberlain during these years of waiting and after she became Mrs Garrington she preferred to use her maiden name in her professional work.

John had to obtain permission from the Church of England establishment in order to marry *Reverend* Elsie Chamberlain; there would have been no objections to him marrying *Miss* Elsie Chamberlain. It seems that opposition to the proposed marriage was based purely on doctrinal grounds. The Church of England does not ordain women as priests. The authorities thought that Elsie was trying to gain entry to the priesthood by marrying an Anglican curate! This was totally untrue, since Elsie was then, and remained throughout her life, a staunch Congregationalist.

Officials in high places let it be known that they did not

consider a marriage between the Rev John Garrington and the Rev Elsie Chamberlain to be suitable. It was considered that if John was given a parish his wife would be expected to be his support and help wholly in his parish. His wife should be confirmed .Obstacles were placed in the way of John Garrington. He found it very difficult to progress from being a curate to being a priest. Throughout his subsequent priesthood John never had much preferment and it seems probable that he was never forgiven for marrying a nonconformist minister. It was felt that Elsie, being an ordained Free Church minister, could not devote one hundred per cent to the duties required of a vicar's wife. She would be ministering to her own church members and thereby serving two masters.

Elsie's mother did not approve of the match between John and her daughter. There seems to be no reason why she objected. John wrote, after the engagement was broken, 'The fact that your Ma is inclined to bully, without evidence or prompting, doesn't say much for her sanity! Since daughters often take after their fathers and he is weak willed, make me wonder why on earth I still want to marry you.'

Although Elsie had broken off her engagement to John Garrington in 1941, he was very persistent. He pursued her ardently and never accepted the broken engagement. In letters written between 1942–1946, which Elsie kept, John often refers to Elsie as 'my own darling wife.' He never questioned that one day Elsie would become his wife.

Elsie made it clear that she wanted to marry and have a family. She would not contemplate marriage until John had a living. Throughout the early forties John continued his quest for a living. He applied for many posts, some advertised and others suggested by friends, but the vacancies, mysteriously, became 'unavailable'.

In 1943, John wrote to Elsie, 'I'm glad you are sorry I lost that place because I am. Still, I've got busy and applied for two temporary jobs; one in Guernsey and one in Falmouth. Also for a vicarage in Dunnow. This is only a small thing but vacancies are hard to find in London now.'

In another letter, dated June 1944, John was exasperated. He wrote 'The job at Birmingham is off, the Chester job has not materialized, nor have I heard from Shrewsbury. I have applied for another two posts, one in Canterbury and one in Gloucester. I want desperately to settle down to a job and marry you.'

Elsie felt she should help John's cause by personally intervening. She wrote to the Bishop of London, who at that time was the Bishop responsible for John. She went to see Dr Wand and at the meeting promised to give up her pastorate, and possible confirmation was discussed. This was followed up with a letter. Here is the gist of correspondence that passed between Elsie and Dr Wand.

FULHAM PALACE, S.W.6.

15 October 1945.

Dear Miss Chamberlain,

    I am very glad to have your letter saying that you will resign your pastorate on marrying John Garrington. May I wish you every happiness and a long life together.

    With regard to confirmation you are probably wise to wait a little. I hope you will find some sympathetic priest who will be able to point out for you the Anglican position more fully than I could do at our interview. Of course you know enough already and have far greater intellectual grasp than 99% of our candidates for confirmation but the more important point is the disposition brought by the candidate. There ought to be a complete readiness to accept whatever is involved in the service with the heart as well as with the mind and there is such a thing as an Anglican ethos with which I am sure you will want to become thoroughly familiar.

        With all good wishes,
        Yours sincerely,

        + Wm: London.

Miss E. D. Chamberlain.

---

10 December 1945.

Dear Miss Chamberlain,

I am sorry to have been rather slow in
answering your letter but I wanted to give it proper
consideration. I do not wonder that you are a little
worried and I should like to help you in any way I can.
The matter is not as easy as it appears at first sight.
While it is true that there is a dearth of clergy there
is as a matter of fact no dearth of incumbents. The
gaps are in the ranks of the juniors not of the seniors.
With all these chaplains coming back from the Forces we
shall certainly have a bad bottleneck in this diocese,
otherwise I would say that he could easily get a living in
this diocese. I certainly should not stand in his way
in view of the agreement we came to in our recent correspondence; but I can quite realise as I pointed out to you
then that in view of the peculiar circumstances other
patrons might feel some hesitation. I am quite sure that
John is not imagining or inventing obstacles. They are
there all right but I feel sure they can be overcome on
the lines that we laid down together.

You ask for my advice. The only definite
advice that I can give you is that you should not tie
yourself up with any further work which it would not be
possible for you to drop at once if John got his appointment and marriage proved possible. It would be very hard
lines on you both if you suddenly found the way become open
but you had put yourself in some moral obligation which
closed the door again.

In the meantime you may reply upon me to
look around and see whether anything can be done; but John
ought to go on making his own enquiries. If he finds
a possible opening I am quite prepared to back him. I
should very much like to see you married and settled
down in a post where you could both be happy.

Yours sincerely,

+ Wm: London:

Dear Doctor Wand,

Forgive my plain speaking or writing. I feel sure that you would admit that my impressions of the Church of England working, are a mixed bag. It's apparently unfortunate for every one concerned that I'm so fond of John Garrington. I don't think we had better marry till he is appointed – as until that actually happens, I shall be afraid someone will doublecross us. As for the alternative, I'm a minister – and if I feel I can fulfil my ministry as John's wife, we shall be married one day, I hope. My idea of marriage is for the purpose of raising a family and if we wait much longer that will be gone.

FULHAM PALACE, S.W.6.

18 December 1945.

Dear Miss Chamberlain,

        I discussed the contents of your letter with the Staff ~~committee~~ at our meeting yesterday. Everyone was sympathetic although all are agreed that it would be impossible for John to be appointed to one of our posts while you were still serving your Free Church Pastorate.
        The Bishop of Kensington is actually trying to get John a post in connection with Toc H. From that he would ~~ultimately~~ get a living, but I imagine that in the meantime the stipend would not be enough to marry on. Would it be possible for us to find you some kind of secretarial post, or would you be able to find some post for yourself? Together, you might earn enough to start a home on, although I realise to the full the unsatisfactory nature of such an arrangement. Perhaps you will let me know what you think about this.

        Yours sincerely,

        + Wm: London:

41

21.12.45

Dear Doctor Wand,

Your letter of the 18th December, arrived in time to give me a very unhappy background for Christmas. I sometimes think the only solution to our problem is not to marry. If I promise not to marry John, will someone let him get on with the work he feels called to do? Anglican autocracy is becoming a sort of blackmail to which I really cannot subscribe. I am certainly weary of waging war against that sort of holy blackmail. I imagine if you wring from me the promise that I won't marry John, he may be given a living? I've carried on with the great hope for reunion – but most of the Church of England has evidently neither the vision nor the desire for it. I don't call what John is offered 'functioning as an active priest.' I promised you in a previous letter, that you acknowledged, that I would resign my patorate if I married John – if he were in a position to keep us both. You can't possibly mean that in spite of that promise, a possible living would be withheld from him on the grounds of his connection with me which isn't even a formal engagement – that was broken off years ago!

There seems to be livings for people who are not being blackmailed but our only solution seems that I must give up my pastorate before John is given a living. I've only just turned down a very congenial secretarial post at £450 per annum. There is no point in planning a business woman's marriage as, having waited so long, the particular hurry is that I am nearly thirty-six and the prospect of a family becomes more remote. We can't have a family on 'guinea pigging' nor while I am helping to earn the bread and butter, can we?

January 5th, 1946.

My dear Miss Chamberlain,

I certainly did not intend to convey the impression that John would not be appointed to anything until you had resigned your pastorate. He is as eligible for a living at the moment as any other man, but I understand that you on your part are prepared to resign your pastorate if you marry him while he is functioning as an active priest in the Church of England. My letter was only intended to hand on to you the suggestions made by the Staff towards an early fulfilment of your desires. Suitable livings cannot be found at a moment's notice, and the suggestions made were to be regarded as interim proposals until a more permanent settlement could be found.

Thankyou for your most interesting booklet of B.B.C.Talks.

Yours sincerely,

+ Wm; Londin:

Dear Doctor Wand,

I was grateful to have your reassurance and appreciated it tremendously. I must admit having got into a somewhat sensitive state about things. Having discovered some substance in the barriers and difficulties that I thought were shadows, I now see them everywhere.

I am convinced that people are helped to find God under my Ministry. Your staff would prefer that I help out John Garrington's starvation wage in any way I can but the ministry. The only grounds for marriage, from my point of view, is that I can minister as his wife, as fully as I can single – until he has a church I am to be anything rather than a minister.

She took up her appointment as a chaplain. John, however, did not give up. He went to see Dr Wand in person and at this meeting he was told plainly, 'You have no chance whatever of becoming a vicar while you remain

43

engaged to that welfare officer.'

Lord Stansgate heard about Elsie's dilemma. He had struggled with the Church of England establishment over the RAF chaplaincy question and now took a personal interest in the problems of Elsie's proposed marriage. He approached his friend, Lord Jowitt, the Lord Chancellor, who had certain livings in his gift. Within a few days John was offered a living at All Saints' Church in Hampton, Middlesex. John said that he was not sure of the living even then until he was finally instituted on 5 May 1946.

By November 1946 Elsie had been struck down with arthritis. She was quite sure that the prospect of a marriage at last helped with her recovery. She was able to plan for the wedding, thus taking her mind off the unpleasant, painful complaint.

John and Elsie were finally married on 19 July 1947, ten years after their engagement. John was in the position of publishing his own marriage banns and issuing himself a certificate that 'no impediment has been alleged.'

They were married in Elsie's parish church in Friern Barnet. The wedding day was very hot. John's best man was the Rev Robert (Wally) Horth, who had been a fellow student at Kings' College and was now vicar of Shalford, near Guildford, Surrey. John wore a dark grey lounge suit and his clerical collar. He had an apricot-coloured rose in his buttonhole. Elsie was given away by her father, Jim Chamberlain. She wore a simple white linen suit which she had made herself (a reminder of dress-designing days), and a large white straw hat which the chief chaplain had helped her to choose. She also wore white sandals and white gloves. John bought her a string of pearls and sent them to her with a message, 'All my love, darling, yours completely John.' Elsie didn't carry a bouquet. She wore a corsage of red carnations. Years later I was told she wanted a bouquet of red roses but in July 1947 roses were out of season! When I was married in *January* 1964 and carried a bouquet of red roses Elsie was quite envious! She had no bridesmaids. The Rev Prebendary A. E. Dunn, vicar of St James's Church,

This article appeared in the *Daily Sketch*:

Wedding Reception To Last Six Years

The Rev. John Leslie St. Clair Garrington and the Rev. Elsie Dorothea Chamberlain, to be married at Friern Barnet, Middlesex, next month, will have a wedding reception lasting six years.

During their combined 20 years' service in the Church, they have made many more friends than can be entertained at a single reception. So they will be at home once a month to 20 friends. In six years they will receive 1,440.

Muswell Hill, officiated at the service. The church was filled with friends and well-wishers. People and cars reached the church in a steady stream, long before the start of the service. Two policemen had to deal with the resulting traffic jam!

Elsie, still recovering from arthritis, hobbled down the aisle. She was supported by John throughout most of the service. There was so much publicity about an Anglican priest marrying the first woman chaplain in the Forces that John and Elsie left the church through a throng of pressmen and others with cameras. Their marriage made headline news both in this country and abroad.

The reception for family and friends, which included the Stansgates, was a family affair. It took place in the garden at Elsie's home in Friern Barnet. The only mishap happened with the wedding cake. This was a splendid three-tiered construction and had been placed in the bathroom to keep it cool. As it was moved to the garden the cake accidently broke. Fortunately the cake maker was at hand and she did a hurried job to make it the grand centre piece that was intended. (Sixteen years later, this same lady made my wedding cake and it was a replica of Elsie's.)

Elsie managed to save two tiers of her cake for two of these 'reception years'. The wedding reception ended with a violent thunderstorm. At this point John and Elsie took off for their honeymoon. They spent the first week at the vicarage of Wally Horth, their best man, and the second week at a hotel in Torquay. The second part of the honeymoon was a present from her father.

Whilst they were in Torquay they were recognized by a young boy who insisted on taking their photograph and who asked for an autograph!

Most people marvelled at how persistent John and Elsie had been in their fight to be married. John received an anonymous letter signed 'from one who is disgusted'. The writer found it horrible to contemplate such a union and concluded, 'You ought to be unfrocked!'

Years later Elsie and John met Archbishop Fisher and his wife at a Lambeth Palace garden party. Mrs Fisher knew Elsie well and laughingly asked if she was at the function in

Sign—Countersign

AN application for passports by the Rev. John Garrington and his wife, the Rev. Elsie Garrington, set passport officials a poser to-day. Each had witnessed the other's application form.

He is vicar of All Saints, Hampton, and his wife—better known by her maiden name of Chamberlain — is minister of Vineyard Congregational Church, Richmond.

Their claim that as ministers of religion they could sign each other's papers was parried by a passport officer. " Marriage," he said, " makes you sacramentally one, therefore you are really signing for yourself."

The bearded, 36-year-old Rev John. however, after pointing out the distinction between his office as vicar and his marital relationship, won the day.

This report appeared in the *Evening News*, dated 28 March 1948.
What a couple of ministers can get away with!

> 3 Esplanade
> Somerton
> South Australia
> August 20' 1947
>
> Dear Mr + Mrs Garrington,
>   This photo appeared in our newspaper a few
> weeks ago. "The Advertiser", + I thought it might
> interest you to see it.
>   You both seem to be finding life a great joke, + I
> do hope it will continue to be so, for you both.
> In fact your humour has infected me also, + I have
> a laugh every time I look at the photo.
>   Don't be surprised if I send a small parcel next
> time I go to town, every little helps in the way of food
> these days + you must all be having an awful
> time.
>   What a pity Mr Churchill is not still at the head of
> things. England would never have been in this mess
> had he been still in office.
>   Good luck to you both, + do go on laughing.
>   Sincerely yours
>   (Mrs) M. Hodge
>
> You'll be surprised to receive this from a stranger, but I
> just thought it'd be nice to send it along.

As I pointed out John and Elsie's wedding was headline news both in England and abroad. Some kind person sent this letter and clip all the way from Australia. The clip is reproduced in the central photograph section.

her capacity as the Rev Elsie Chamberlain or as Mrs Garrington. Also laughing, the Archbishop said, 'I tried to keep them apart!'

Elsie had finally been accepted by the Church of England establishment!

John made this comment regarding his marriage to Elsie: 'Because of Anglican Church prejudice against women clergy, we had to wait ten years before my bishop could be persuaded to let us marry. We did get married, defying two biases – against women clergy and against closer Anglican/ Congregational relations. We were really pioneers in the matter of church unity. We did it in the teeth of authority.'

Annie
Chamberlain
(née Hayward),
Elsie's mother.

James (Jim)
Chamberlain,
Elsie's father.

Elsie, aged six months

Brothers Ronald and Sidney hold their baby sister, 'Ithe Erl'.

Elsie, Christmas, 1912.

Elsie's birthplace – 30 Canonbury, Park North, Islington, London.
A young Elsie stands in the gateway.

Elsie, aged fifteen.

A family group. Left to Right: Back Row: Sidney and Aunt Ellen, Middle Row: Annie, Gertie, Sidney's wife, and Grandmother. Front Row: Elsie, with cat and Aunt Alice.

The Chamberlain family. Left to Right — Ronald, Mother, Father, Elsie and Sidney.

Islington Chapel where Elsie spent much of her spare time as a child, teenager and young lady. The minister, the Rev Robert Shepherd, inspired Elsie to become a minister.

ISLINGTON CHAPEL
(CONGREGATIONAL)
Corner of Upper Street and Gaskin Street

Having fun at the Islington Chapel.

Miss E.D. Chamberlain (seen with her mother) is studying for a ministerial degree. Prejudice keeps women out, she says. This photo was taken in 1939.

King's College   Faculty of Theology

1936-1937

Elsie   John   Messrs Langfier (6344)

Elsie was told 'There is no guarantee that if we train you for the ministry, you will be considered for a pastorate. You should provide yourself with an alternative means of livelihood.' Elsie was undeterred. 'If that happens I'll go back to dress designing,' she said.

Associate of King's College, London. Ordained in 1937, to St. Martin's Kensal Rise. Appointed St. Saviour's, Chelsea, 1939

J. L. Garrington.

Photograph of Elsie's fiancé, the Rev John Garrington, taken in 1937.

Photographic Agencies Ltd, (7–75)

Squadron officer and chaplain Rev Elsie Chamberlain.

Planet News Ltd

Pre-wedding photo of the Rev John Garrington and the Rev Elsie Chamberlain, taken in the garden of 46 Hathey Close, Friern Barnet. They were engaged for ten years and could have married soon after they first met if Elsie had abandoned her plans for a career in the church, 'but I was set on becoming a minister,' she said.

Newly-weds John and Elsie Garrington, with their
best man, Rev Robert (Wally) Horth.

Vicar Marries Woman Chaplain

The first marriage of an Anglican priest to a Congregational minister was solemnised at the Church of St. John the Evangelist, Friern Barnet, London, recently. The bridegroom was the Rev. John Leslie St. Clair Garrington, 35, vicar of All Saints' Church, Hampton, Middlesex; his bride, the Rev. Elsie Chamberlain, 36, the first woman chaplain to the forces and, until recently, a squadron officer in the WAAF. Before her war service she was minister of Christchurch Congregational Church, Friern Barnet, and she is contemplating taking charge of another church after the marriage. Photo shows the bride and bridegroom leaving after their wedding ceremony.

News clip from The Advertiser, Adelaide, South Australia, dated 19th July, 1947.

Newly ordained minister Rev Elsie Chamberlain. She retained her maiden name in her professional work because she was already well established as such before she married in 1947.

The only surviving photograph of the Garrington family, taken in 1956, in Davos, Switzerland.

Ivor Ashmore, Odhams Press

John and Elsie's marriage was built on love, respect and understanding. It formed a happy partnership which benefited both ministries.

John (Garry) and myself. I adored him.

Ivor Ashmore, Odhams Press

Elsie and I made the most of our precious time together. Here I am helping with the curtain making and having a rare chance for a chat at the same time.

John and Elsie shared a passion for sketching – they were both accomplished artists. John encouraged Elsie to paint 'helps her to relax' he said.

Rev Elsie Chamberlain, 1956.

Greensted Rectory was Elsie's favourite home.

One of John and Elsie's hobbies was to buy houses in need of renovation. Here Elsie is painting the window frame of 'Gable End', their first purchase. We spent many happy weekends and holidays here.

Photograph courtesy of the BBC

Rev Elsie Chamberlain seated at her desk in her BBC office. You can see the 'rubbed mural' in the background.

James Jarche

Rev Elsie Chamberlain, producer of 'Lift up your hearts'.

Elsie's father, Jim Chamberlain, who died, aged 83, in April, 1956.

Elsie's mother, Annie Chamberlain, who died, aged 97, in September, 1975.

The central service of the Women's World Day of Prayer, 1962. –
H.M. Queen Elizabeth, the Queen Mother, seen entering the Church
of St. Martin-in-the-Fields, London, with the Rev Elsie Chamberlain.

John and Elsie at home in the lounge at Greensted Rectory.

Foundation of the Congregational Federation ceremony. Elsie (centre) and Lady Stansgate hold 'the charter'. Lady Stansgate was its first president and the first layman to hold a major position in any church.
Founder Member and Congregational Centre Church secretary, Mr John Wilcox, is on the left of the photograph.

The first woman to take the daily service, Rev Elsie Chamberlain, seen here with other presenters at the Sixtieth Anniversary service in 1988.

West Essex Gazette

Elsie enjoyed a good joke. She had a keen sense of humour and her laugh could 'shake a building'.

John Garrington, born 7th May, 1912, died 28th January, 1978.

Rev Elsie
Chamberlain, born
3rd March, 1910, died
10th April, 1991,
aged 81.

5

Mr and Mrs Garrington

This chapter is about John and Elsie and it concentrates on their homes and marriage.

'I intend to be the best vicar's wife ever,' says the bride of Rev John Garrington.

John and Elsie were complete opposites, both physically and temperamentally. Elsie was a good looking lady, tall and slim. Her hair was dark brown and wavy. She never had her hair cut. She could actually sit on it and as a child I was quite envious of it! She always wore her hair coiled in a braid at the back of her head – I don't remember Elsie having another hairstyle. John, on the other hand, was short and tubby. He had very large and penetrating brown eyes. He had grown a beard in the early forties, as a result of neuralgia. He was a heavy smoker and had a liking for pink gin. Elsie was a staunch teetotaler. Unlike Elsie, John was not very musical or sporty. He was Welsh and he did have a very clear singing voice. Both had a sense of humour and their laughs could shake a building!

The vicarage at Hampton was Elsie's first matrimonial home. John had lived there as a bachelor, one year before his marriage. It was a detached, double-fronted house. The inner rooms were small. Attached to the house was a very large garden, mostly grass and mature trees. Elsie didn't like housework – she never really had to keep house. Housework and cooking were not a priority to her. A parishioner used to come and clean. John's study, situated downstairs, was near to immaculate, since most visitors to the vicarage were shown into that room. The lounge, sometimes called the music room, was rarely used. I was responsible for keeping my bedroom clean and tidy and that was always in a perfect state!

When John and Elsie finally married in 1947, he was thirty-five and she was thirty-seven. They took a joint decision not to have children of their own but to adopt. Elsie had by then decided against a life of domestic bliss and to pursue her strong vocational calling. She had also suffered a very serious illness. They decided to adopt a child rather than a baby. They also wanted to adopt a child who had been born during the war years, since that might have been the age of their own offspring had they married when planned. Elsie said she could only cope with one child – so she had the choice of the number and the age! John chose the sex of the child.

My guardians were the British Legion and they were seeking a family to foster me. Just after their marriage Elsie was called to the ministry at the Vineyard Congregational Church in Richmond, Surrey. Round the corner from this church was a children's home run by the British legion, for the children of ex-servicemen. Some of the children's fathers had been killed in action and some fathers had returned from the battlefields wounded. I was a very quiet child who preferred to do things on my own. I was considered 'intelligent'. I have never enjoyed sport, PE or games and I have an innate fear of swings, fairs, climbing, jumping and many other childish pursuits. I hate sudden and loud noises. I was tall for my age and scrawny, a terrible giggler and keen Brownie. All the 'home' children attended Elsie's church, regardless of their family roots and religion. I remember meeting John for the first time. He had come to judge a Brownie competition at Elsie's Church. He took an immediate shine to me; he found me interesting, intelligent and full of fun. But Elsie's reaction to me was quite different: 'That thing, she's a mouse'. John took a great deal of interest in me and Elsie began to notice 'the mouse'. She realized that I was a great favourite with John. It was John

50

who picked 'the child'. At first I went to stay with John and Elsie for weekends and then I was fostered on a full-time basis. John wanted to make my position more permanent and he made enquiries with a view to legal adoption. This was acceptable to the British legion. Thus I became the adopted daughter of John and Elsie Garrington. My surname was changed to theirs. I was chosen and regarded as their child.

Elsie had her study upstairs. The vicarage was built before the days when central heating was a standard feature. Elsie was a cold mortal, so she had a tiny box room for her study, which also housed the airing cupboard and faced south-east. Elsie had lived through two world wars and a general strike. She had been taught to be thrifty to the point that she never threw anything away, particularly paper. Her study was always a mess and I marvelled at how she ever found important papers and letters. Occasionally one of John's parishioners would act as secretary.

Elsie could never resist a bargain, likewise John! Elsie would go to salerooms and buy pieces of furniture, crockery and furnishings at rock bottom prices. The vicarage was full of furniture and furnishings. Often the furniture bought was big and bulky and totally unsuited to the small-sized rooms. When my future husband came to the house, he had to walk in sideways to squeeze past all the furniture in the hallway! The downstairs cloakroom was even worse, as this, at one time, housed six mowers, extra ironing boards and deckchairs. As for John's bargains, they were quite inexplicable. He once bought a lorry load of oak wood, used for making beer barrels. This was dumped in the garden and there it remained for years!

John was an avid reader and he loved books. His study was shelved from floor to ceiling to accommodate books, mostly purchased secondhand. John was also a very keen and first class photographer. He had a small darkroom upstairs where he could develop and print his photographs. Elsie was keen on making things. She made a lot of her own clothes. She would buy up tatty chairs and recover them –

51

the trouble was that she rarely finished recovering one chair, sofa or pouffe before she embarked on another one! She never seemed to have time to complete or she lost interest in them because she hated doing 'fiddly bits'. Elsie did make some of my clothes but preferred to buy them 'on my behalf'. Her choice was not mine. This problem was solved by John who gave me a clothes allowance. Then I was able to buy clothes of my choice and what I considered to be fashionable. According to Elsie I had no dress sense and now when I look at contemporary photographs of myself, I'm inclined to agree with her! When the housework seemed to be piling up uncomfortably, then we would have a field day, doing household chores. It was lucky that neither John nor Elsie were houseproud. The clutter and mess never worried them. It was their home and it was a place they could relax in!

John was a late riser, unless he had an early service. He would go without breakfast. He would survive on a cup of strong, unsweetened, black coffee. It was a family joke that John had his breakfast before retiring to bed. Then he would have fried egg and bacon and extras like tomatoes and mushrooms, when available. This was followed with cheese and biscuits. Elsie never slept well and rose at daylight. She was energetic from dawn to dusk. She enjoyed a good breakfast of lemon juice, cereal and porridge, fruit and yoghurt. She drank very weak tea – preferably herbal. Elsie had a very sweet tooth while John and I took very little sugar. Our meal would consist of soup followed by the main course but no dessert. John wasn't a 'pudding man'. Elsie's great love was bananas, especially if they were brown and mushy. John had been brought up near the sea and loved seafood. Elsie had been brought up in London and found seafood 'suspect'. I remember collecting mussels on one of our holidays. John cooked them in water and devoured them with great relish. We once found a very, very tiny pearl inside one and Elsie was thrilled and kept it for years! John was very handy in the kitchen. He enjoyed making jams and pickles. We had bottles and bottles of fruit! We always said grace before our meals but we didn't have a daily Bible reading.

When Elsie married she entered into the duties of a vicar's wife. She joined the Mothers' Union. She instigated a Young Wives' Club. This was a great success and, as far as I know, still exists but now is just a Wives' Club, opened to young and old! (When Elsie's workload increased it became a joke that when she wanted to leave from a meeting early, she would use the excuse, 'Sorry, I must go and attend to John's Young Wives!')

She helped John in his church activities. The vicarage and garden were available for the annual summer fete. At Christmas time and Easter she would involve 'any singing parishioner' in musical events. She would conduct the big popular oratorios, *Messiah*, *The Creation*, *Elijah*. Anybody who could sing was welcomed to join the chorus. These musical events were popular – there was never a shortage of participants or listeners. She ran a small orchestra for the children of the parish. She would teach them the rudiments of music and instrument technique. Another of Elsie's duties as a vicar's wife was to serve cups of tea or coffee to visitors to the vicarage and act as hostess to visiting clergy. The Bishop of London had dinner with us after a confirmation service, held in John's church. Elsie was at the service. Near the end of the service John gave out an instruction to the congregation, which caused Elsie to laugh out loud! Over dinner the Bishop, John and I found out what Elsie found so hilarious. John's closing announcement was, 'After the Blessing, the Bishop will leave the church and we shall sing the hymn, *Now thank we all our God*'. I should think this story made a good 'after dinner one' for the Bishop! If Elsie was at home and the door or telephone bell rang, it was she who answered. She made John's parishioners welcome. Elsie taught me to iron those dreadful clerical garments, surplices. It was a job she loathed and she thought she was doing a motherly job, teaching me how to iron the wretched things! John always had clean cottas and surplices. That was one of Elsie's priority jobs!

53

John was keen that girls should have the same rights and opportunities as boys. He introduced female servers and girl choristers. I had become an Anglican and was a member of John's church choir. John was broadminded about Christian names. The vicar of a sister parish church refused to christen babies with name derivatives, so Lisa had to be christened Elizabeth, Sally Sarah and so on.

Elsie was very strict on observing Sunday as the 'Lord's Day'. I was banned from doing certain things like homework on Sundays. In fact a lot of tasks were banned and I considered it to be illogical thinking! Fireworks flew one Sunday when I dared to wash my hair! I could not see, then or now, why I could wash my face but not my hair on a Sunday! John took my side in the argument and we were both in the doghouse for days. In the end I had to come to an agreement with John that if I wanted to do something on the 'banned list' it had to be done when Elsie wasn't around!

I spent Coronation Day with some friends. They had bought a television so that they could watch the event in their living room. I was invited for the day. Unfortunately the host family gave me a small drop of champagne to toast the Queen. What was more unfortunate was that I went home bragging that I had had some champagne! Elsie, being a staunch teetotaler, was furious, and I was banned from that household as the adults in it were deemed irresponsible. (I can assure you I only had a thimble full!) John was a Mason and a member of a working man's club and was more tolerant towards drinking alcohol. Elsie had no say in John's drinking habits!

As a teenager I was in awe of Elsie. She really found it hard to cope with me, not that I was difficult or naughty. I was just growing up. When I started to experiment with make-up I had problems. Elsie had been brought up to deplore any form of vanity. John was not so condemning and constantly reminded Elsie that I had to make up my own mind. If I wanted to look like a clown that was my choice! I soon learnt that I needed very little make up since

I have been blessed with a good skin and reasonable hair colour, even now at over fifty!

John and Elsie bought a thatched cottage in Chute, near Andover in Hampshire. They decided to buy a home of their own because the vicarage did not belong to them – it was their home whilst John remained as the incumbent of All Saints' Church, Hampton.

We spent odd days and holidays there. It was furnished with some of the surplus items from the vicarage. Elsie had a wonderful time decorating and furbishing the cottage. Enthusiasm for this cottage was the stimulus to them to purchase other cottages, some of which were very derelict. They obtained grants to modernize these properties into habitable homes.

They had a dream that when they retired they might have an antique shop. This prompted a further round of visits to sales and auctions. Both had field days bidding for clocks, teapots, walking sticks, water bottles and all sorts of bric à brac. You name it, John and Elsie collected it! The cottages and seeking out bargain purchases was wonderful therapy for them both – it was something they could do together with their precious spare time and have fun doing it.

Most of the cottages were disposed of some years ago. One of the cottages, near Plymouth, was used as a consulting room for John's psychiatric work. John was able to hyponotise people and use this gift to try to bring relief to people who had been referred to him with psychological problems. He would delve into their subconscious and try to cure their minds and ailments. He had some success, especially when working with people suffering from asthma and allergies.

John's interest in psychology went back to the days before he was a student, when he worked in his home town of Aberystwyth, in Wales. Here he had access to the psychology library of the local university. When he became a priest John found it difficult to deal with the individual's soul through religion alone. Distraught people need sympathetic counselling or mental treatment alongside

55

religion. John assumed that priests were expected to be amateur psychiatrists because he saw psychiatry as an extension of the confessional.

The role of clergymen had changed and over the years their pastoral work had diminished. The divide between church and the treatment couch had come about at the beginning of this century, when many of the advanced thinkers in the field of psychology were regarded as 'permissive do-gooders'. There was also apathy between the Medical Association and laymen, though this apathy is now beginning to cease because of the advent of public interest in homoeopathy and the use of hypnosis in therapy. People are now more aware of natural remedies and cures and their use in preference to surgery.

Hypnotherapy was one of John's tools because it was a means of getting through to people who had psychiatric troubles, phobias and little will power of their own. Experience had taught John that 'there was always a spiritual background to mental disorder'. He was a staunch believer that mental hospitals should include representation of the clergy among their staff because many of the patients were 'possessed of the devil and that if the soul of the man is distraught, then his mind and body were bound to be also.'

Through hypnotherapy John helped many people – not just his parishioners but also those referred to him by doctors and those who were seeking alternatives to modern medicines. Elsie considered John's work in the field to be 'divine healing'.

In 1963 we moved from Hampton to Greensted, near Ongar in Essex. This was Elsie's favourite home. She loved Greensted Rectory with its spacious rooms and large garden. The garden was overgrown except for a rose bed and it had a stream running through it. Although the rooms were large, they were soon cluttered up with bargain buys! John loved the church at Greensted. It is a historical church. The walls are Saxon and still retain the original log timbers. John made a special effort to encourage appreciation of the building and was overjoyed when it was chosen as part of the 1972 set of postage stamps, commemorating famous British churches. He had new publications produced which told its story. He did a lot of research on those connected with the church in bygone days. John and Elsie encouraged school parties and groups of people to visit the church and both would act as knowledgeable guides. Greensted had a flower festival, as do many other churches. John had this changed to a herb festival. He wrote leaflets to explain how herbs could be used for many purposes. He was always interested in homoeopathy and had little faith in modern remedies. When I was a child and I had a cold, I was given undiluted quinine – ghastly!

The stream which ran through the garden was converted into a watercress bed. They also had a vegetable garden and strawberry bed. Elsie loved strawberries but when the fruits were ripening they mysteriously vanished. Elsie used to get up very early to try to catch the culprits – field mice and birds!

The rectory, in its two acres of grounds, was so quiet that when we had visitors to stay overnight they had problems sleeping – they were used to noises in the night.

I met Leonard Williams and proudly introduced him to John and Elsie. Elsie did not accept Leonard as being a suitable husband because he is a self confessed atheist. Elsie felt that I had snubbed all the ideals of Christianity that she had taught me. John held no such views. It was my prerogative to choose my husband and that his lack of Christian faith did not mean he was unacceptable and that I had relinquished my faith. In fact, Elsie became very fond of her son-in-law. She enjoyed his company and was able to appreciate his good qualities though Leonard would never be drawn into religious discussions with her. He found out very quickly that it was unwise to express a different opinion to hers!

I was married in Greensted Church at Christmas time. John was very disappointed that he did not officiate at my wedding and I hated to disappoint him so. My husband thought that if John had married us I wouldn't have taken my vows seriously! We also had another upset because Leonard (my husband) and his family wanted to serve sherry and wine with the wedding breakfast. This was most definitely vetoed by Elsie who issued an ultimatum, 'Drink or me'. Needless to say I chose Elsie, but after the wedding and when she visited our home, wine was always on the dinner table – Leonard is a great wine maker!

I was always very close to John and this closeness revealed itself in many ways. When I gave birth to my first child, John apparently sat up in bed at two o'clock in the morning and informed Elsie that I was on my way to hospital! He then went back to sleep but on waking he was able to inform Elsie that I had had a boy and that he was about seven and a half pounds and that I had had a very easy labour! To this day I do not know how John knew, except that mentally he was always very close to me. When Colin, my son, was fifteen months old I had a phone call from Elsie. Could she borrow Colin for a photocall for a woman's magazine? It appeared that the magazine was to 'do' an article about her as a family woman. We, as doting parents, were thrilled – we bought Colin a bright red outfit for the occasion and on the day he was a very obliging and photogenic 'angel'. Any rate, when the article was printed, the caption under the photograph read: 'A relaxed moment in Elsie Chamberlain's busy life – time for a word with a young parishioner (Woman's Own 5 November 1966). I was quite upset by this and never understood why her grandson was labelled 'a young parishioner'.

John christened both his grandchildren. Years later, Elsie was thrilled to be able to take part, at our local parish church, in the wedding service of my daughter, Stephanie. It was the last occasion at which Elsie wore her RAF stole and was possibly the last time she participated at an Anglican service in an Anglican church. That was one of the high spots in her last year.

I am terrified of cats and Elsie thought if we had a cat I might overcome my fear. John didn't like cats, but one day a visitor arrived at the rectory in a car. On the back shelf of the car was a sleek Burmese cat. John saw the cat and said, 'I wouldn't mind having at cat like that.' He saw a notice in *The Times*: 'A good home wanted for a Burmese cat'. He made enquiries and got the cat, called Chola. Chola was a beautiful cat but appearances were deceptive, as she was very bad-tempered. This experience only confirmed my fear and then dislike of cats! She was always snapping and snarling and very fussy with her food. John loved the cat and Chola loved John and nobody else! When John and Elsie made their trips to Plymouth, Chola would go in the car with them. She was unrestrained and allowed to roam around the car as Elsie was driving! I was horrified one day when Chola jumped on to the steering wheel. The following Christmas I bought a cat basket so that Chola could be put in it whilst in transit from one place to another. Chola didn't like that idea and would never go into the basket. When Chola died Elsie got another Burmese cat, the granddaughter of Chola, who was a little more amicable.

John didn't drive. He relied on Elsie for transportation. Although Elsie was always in control of the car, driving with her was an experience. Elsie was a chatterbox and would often drive round a roundabout several times because she was in deep conversation. Another unnerving habit she had was actually taking her hands off the steering wheel and turning round to speak to the back passengers.

One day she and John drove over to see us in Gravesend. They spent the day with us and left when it was dark. At 10.30 that same evening John phoned; he was laughing his head off! Eventually I was told that Mother had run into the back of a lorry. I didn't think this was very funny. As far as I know this was the only mishap Elsie had. On this occasion, she had driven into the back of a lorry loaded with beer kegs!

Colin, my son, has a favourite story of when he and his grandmother (Elsie) were driving along a country road when she had to slow down because pigs were being moved from one field to another. She managed to get round the pigs and went on her way. Coming towards her was a police car and she signalled the car to stop. When the two cars were abreast, Elsie put down her window and shouted 'Pigs' and promptly drove off! Then there is the classic story about the time when Elsie parked her car. The road had been coned off but Elsie ignored the cones. The reason the cones were there was because workmen were painting yellow lines. Mother received a summons for parking on yellow lines. She pleaded not guilty and insisted that the yellow lines were painted after she had parked. She won the case!

John and Elsie would discuss together the differences in their Christian outlook. Each supported the other in the separate churches. Before Elsie was able to receive communion in the Church of England she had to obtain permission from the bishop of the diocese. They were both admired by many people in different walks of life. Once we found a large packet on the vicarage doorstep addressed to 'the reverend couple'. When we opened it, it contained £1 and £5 notes. We spent a whole afternoon counting and recounting the money! It was an anonymous gift which was to go to a charity of John and Elsie's choice. We never discovered the identity of the donor but the money found its way to a worthy cause.

Elsie combined being a vicar's wife, housewife and mum. At home and in the parish, she was Mrs Garrington. Admiral F. Clifton Brown said, 'It's a lucky parish that has two "sky pilots" to look after it.' Yet in spite of these parish commitments she was able to follow her vocation as the Rev Elsie Chamberlain. John and Elsie felt 'that when a woman has a true calling for the ministry her sex should not be a barrier to the fulfilment of her vocation.'

6

Elsie and the BBC

One day in May 1950 Elsie's mother saw an advertisement in a newspaper. Two assistant producers were required for the restaffing of the Religious Department at the BBC: 'People with varied experience in the ministry, preferred.' She showed the advertisement to Elsie and urged her to apply for one of the vacancies. Elsie had broadcast in 1945 and her mother thought that this previous experience would give her some advantage.

Elsie applied for one of the posts, as did 2000 other applicants! The Appointments Board found it difficult to prepare a short list and interviewed several groups in the course of two days. Elsie was one of the last interviewees. By the time it came to her turn the appointing board had to all intents and purposes made their selection. Elsie walked into the appointments room and her presence immediately created an impression. The Rev. Francis House, then the Head of Religious Broadcasting, whispered to his neighbour, 'She knows how to dress.' She was told that two applicants had, more or less, already been selected, so she needed to convince the board that they needed *three* new producers! She was successful and three new producers were appointed: Rev. Richard (Dick) Tatlock, who had been a naval chaplain; Mr J. Ormerod Greenwood, a radio dramatist; Rev. Elsie Chamberlain, a Congregational minister. Mr Greenwood and Elsie were to work on a part-time basis. Elsie was the first *ordained* woman producer in the Religious Department. She took up her appointment in July 1950.

61

Elsie's duties included taking responsibility for *Lift Up Your Hearts*, a short broadcast every weekday morning with an estimate of three million listeners. She was to be responsible for planning the schedule for these broadcasts throughout the year and to supervise their scripts. Secondly, she was to take responsibility for a fifteen minute programme for missionaries, broadcast on the Overseas Service, once a fortnight. Thirdly, she was asked to help from time to time in the production of outside broadcasts of services from the London area. This meant attending the rehearsal or congregational practice on a Friday evening or Saturday afternoon. Fourthly, because she was an ordained member of staff, she should be available to conduct a late Saturday evening service about once every three months and *The Daily Service* once a week. Once a week there would be an internal staff meeting at which future plans were discussed and when the previous week's programmes were criticized. This was an extensive contract for a part-time appointment. Elsie took it in her stride, and she loved the work. Five years later her contract was given full-time status as from 1 January 1955.

Lift Up Your Hearts is the programme most people associate with Elsie. She entered into it with the enthusiasm of a missionary. The programme was live and Elsie left home at 6 am every morning. Through the wireless set she was able to enter homes anywhere in the British Isles, and open the Bible where otherwise it would never be read. She had a congregation of three million people of whom three quarters never went to church. Her aim was to introduce ordinary people to Christianity and not to one particular denomination; the idea that attracted her most was the opportunity to 'win the ear of people on the fringes of the Church and those to whom religion was only a word, and not a very interesting word at that!' She aimed to give people something that would be a Christian message, to think about during the day.

Every week some well-known person, cleric or layman, was invited to give a short talk each morning for a week's duration. It was Elsie's job to get the great preachers to modify their pulpit style and to encourage them to 'chat to one person'. It was difficult to put on a programme that appealed to every one of a multitude of people of differing backgrounds, social strata and education. Elsie would delete from her guests' scripts unnecessary adjectives and adverbs. She discouraged theological ideas and dogma. Scripts had to be simple so that the message could be understood by ordinary people.

Elsie had a letter from one listener, congratulating her on her 'plain and simple approach'. Elsie knew the value of the right word in the right place. She always had a steady stream of correspondence; some praised while others criticized. When the hymn *The Wise may Bring Their Learning* was sung to an unfamiliar tune, the BBC was inundated with telephone calls asking what the tune was. At home we had a placard placed by the telephone so that John and I could answer the enquiry too! I remember when Elsie had a speaker who started his broadcast each day with a nursery rhyme. This caused a furore of praise and criticism. What appealed to some tastes was poison to others! Elsie had a series of speakers who had experienced a wonderful cure through faith. This stimulated a lot of criticism, as people could not understand why, in spite of their faith and prayers, others had not been cured of their sickness.

Once, when Elsie answered her office telephone, she had her rubber in her hand and whilst listening and talking, she decided to clean her rubber on the wall! The call was quite lengthy and by the time it finished, Elsie had made a sizeable clean patch on a rather grubby BBC wall! For several weeks she spent her lunch break trying to hide the prominent patch. She did this by drawing, with her rubber, a mural of 'Jacob's Dream'. The wall no longer looked grubby and it became a talking point and was much admired by visitors! Whether the mural still exists I don't know, but a press photographer took a picture of Elsie sitting at her desk with the 'rubbed mural', complete with ladder and ascending angel, in the background. Elsie had a

63

reputation for being reliable and able to handle a crisis. 'A good producer – the best in the department,' said one colleague.

Lift up your hearts also went out on the overseas network. Many of these listeners regarded Elsie as a personal friend. Her other overseas programme, *Work and Worship*, was a special one particularly aimed at missionaries. Their children, at schools in England, sent messages to their parents via this programme.

Elsie was the first woman to lead *The Daily Service*. After her initial broadcast some people wrote to say that in their opinion the blessing should not be given by a woman. It was felt by some that only men could bless! Elsie felt such letters came from 'diehard anti-feminists'. Her friend and colleague, Rev. Edwin Robertson, said, 'She was a woman's voice in a male reserve'. However, some people loved having a woman taking the service and on page 65 are two letters in praise of her.

Sometimes *The Saturday Night Prayers* programme was postponed until after the news and then the speaker would conclude the evening's broadcasting. After one service, conducted by Elsie, someone asked, 'Who is that woman who comes on after the transmitter is switched off?' Here is another statement published as part of a letter in a national daily newspaper: 'Then of course we have the lady preacher telling us how to go into retreat.' Elsie had the respect of many of the great preachers of the fifties and sixties, of many different denominations and faiths, and of other producers. Stuart Hibberd, who at one time compered *Silver Lining*, was with others in a studio in Exeter whilst Elsie was 'producing' from one in London. Somehow the wires were crossed. The London studio was internally linked to the Exeter one and conversations taking place in Exeter could be heard in London. Stuart Hibberd commented, 'There is a woman producing today,' thinking that might explain the technical hitch! Elsie had a high regard for Stuart Hibberd, who 'taught her to use her voice'.

Elsie was trained for television. She did not like the

64

Daily Mirror 22 February 1957

medium for religious broadcasting because she felt that 'television was for demonstration and entertainment'. She thought it a problem to know what to put on a screen during a religious talk. Pictures relating to the subject matter were usually too distracting. There was always a danger that some people might be too busy looking at the speaker's profile, instead of listening to what is being said. 'There are very few faces that will bear staring at in close-up for some twenty minutes on end.' I remember once when Elsie returned home, having been on the television, that I remarked, 'You do look nice!' The make-up artist always put on a thick layer of make-up which Elsie loathed. She spent ages washing it off and did not take kindly to my offer of my bottle of Anne French Cleansing Milk!

Elsie was a regular contributor on *Woman's Hour*. She talked to women about religious problems, advised on the religious upbringing of children, recommended books which were worth reading and answered many letters. In January 1956 Elsie received a communication from the Rev. J. M. Elphinstone-Fyffe, a BBC colleague, as a result of a programme called *Talk it over*: 'Congratulations! This establishes your position as the pin-up of the Religious Broadcasting Department.' *Talk it over* was a TV programme and part of *Woman's Hour*.

Elsie worked for the BBC for about seventeen years. In her notes she writes, 'I don't know why I was sacked.' However, correspondence between her and the Religious Department of the BBC, written at the time, makes it clear that there were differences in outlook. Firstly, Elsie refused to attend her annual interview and secondly, the department felt that there was a need for a new 'younger' style of presentation in *Lift Up Your Hearts*, a view Elsie did not share. She attended her interview after pleas had been made, and after consultation with colleagues. The atmosphere at the interview was very frosty. Elsie was told that 'any programme which has been on the air continuously for so long, needs to be given a fresh impetus and new look'. Elsie felt that her value to the department was not exhausted and she still had many ideas for programmes which she wished to promote. She also felt that she had not been given sufficient encouragement and had even urged at staff meetings for less time to be spent discussing past programmes and to allow more time to consider future programmes. Elsie was finally reconciled to the view that as *Lift Up Your Hearts* was being axed, then it's producer was no longer required. She resigned. Michael Standing, Controller, Programme Organization (Sound) wrote, 'I am exceedingly sorry that matters have developed in this way because we are warmly and genuinely appreciative of the work you have done.'

Elsie's departure from the BBC was an unhappy one. She had loved her 'missionary' work. She was, without doubt, a very good producer. Many listeners wrote to Elsie to express their regret. Some women were concerned that the

66

With many thanks for all your
help with Home This Afternoon.
May all your linings be silver!

Jack Singleton

In gratitude + affection,
recalling many years of happy collaboration,
+ recalling, too, the inspiration that
your work has given me.

Agnellus.

For friendship and
much wisdom – many thanks
and all good wishes
John Elphinstone-Fyffe

67

With gratitude for your great contribution
to our common task, as well as the
friendship and fellowship we have
enjoyed, and with affection ever.
KB.

I will miss you in the Studios.
It was fun working with & knowing,
You. Michael Harlamp

With happy memories
of many studio epics
— Good luck
Henry Kuttner.

I shall always remember that it was you
who launched me so happily into broadcasting.
For this and much else I shall always be
grateful to you.

Ray Trevivian

Warmest esteem and affection — tinged with regret —

Adrian Carey

With every good wish, sorry to be losing you
from 'our' end of the corridor

John Stapleton

Many thanks for all your help and
kindness over the years — and for all those
splendid Lift-Ups, especially. We shall miss
you in the Langham.
All the best to John and yourself.

Hubert.

Langham 4468
Broadcasts London-W1
Telex 22182

BROADCASTING HOUSE

LONDON W.1

30th January 1967

Dear Miss Chamberlain,

I know that you are not very happy about the circumstances of your departure from the BBC. Nevertheless, I beg you to allow me to send you this word of very real gratitude for the contribution you have made over these many years to religious broadcasting. We have been very conscious of the dedication with which you have pursued your work in the BBC, and of the high purposes you have always set yourself. Apart from the professional side, I would like you to be assured that your colleagues have always held you in high affection and regard, and at the personal level you will be much missed.

May I be permitted to wish you the very best of good fortune and success in whatever you decide to undertake in the next chapter.

Yours sincerely,

Frank Gillard

(Frank Gillard)
Director of Sound Broadcasting

Rev. E.D. Chamberlain,
Room 82,
Langham.

ABT

Religious Department of the BBC might become a male reserve sphere. They had assurances from the Director General that 'In planning the future staffing of the Department we shall not lose sight of the fact that the qualities needed for this work may be found amongst women as well as men.'

When Elsie retired from the BBC, she was given an autograph book, containing many signed messages of appreciation by her colleagues. Many wished her well for the future and hoped they would meet her again. A selection from the book is reproduced on the preceding pages.

However, this was not quite the end of Elsie's BBC career. She continued to broadcast her scripts on BBC Radio Nottingham's, *Thought For the Day*, and was writing scripts for them until her death. She was regarded as a real professional at work. And in 1988, Elsie was the guest of honour on the occasion of the sixtieth anniversary broadcast of *The Daily Service* from the church of All Souls, Langham Place, London.

'Elsie of the BBC' was not forgotten. She had become a household name and many churchgoers, who saw her name as visiting preacher or minister on the public display boards, came to enquire of her. They personally thanked her for the happy memories of the fine contribution she gave to British religious broadcasting.

After her death, the BBC paid tribute to Elsie, which was much appreciated by her family and many admirers: 'For many, she was the symbol of the place women were beginning to occupy in the public ministry of the churches in post war years. A Congregational Minister, making history in 1946 as the first woman chaplain to the Forces; making history, too, as the first woman presenter of *The Daily Service* on BBC Radio, where she worked in religious broadcasting for almost thirty years.'

7

Who Is To Say Only Men Have A Strong Enough Vocation To Enter The Priesthood?

Elsie believed very strongly that 'God calls people to do specific jobs and that it is against the will of God if there are restrictions against women. Becoming a priest or minister has nothing to do with sex, it has to do with inner convictions.'

In 1946 Elsie broke all precedents when she was appointed a chaplain in the RAF. During the Second World War a committee of women asked the Archbishop of Canterbury to discuss the question of the spiritual welfare of women in the Forces. The Archbishop, together with the heads of all churches and women's services, decided the committee had a valid point and this resulted in the appointment of district organizers for all women's forces. It was later suggested to the War Office that women might work as chaplains' assistants in the army. Their duties were restricted to taking informal discussions and assisting in services, visiting those in hospitals, taking the padre's hour for women and generally to assist him. Elsie's appointment as a chaplain allowed her to lead prayers, act as padre to men and women and take services. Elsie said, 'The lads pulled my leg at first and thought up all kinds of nicknames – but after the nine day-wonder had worn off, they treated me like any other chaplain.'

She also felt that one of the principle duties of any clergyman was listening to the troubles of those in difficulty. She always felt, and particularly in the RAF, that most people found it easier to talk to a woman than to a man.

The ministry is one of the few professions in which women are in the minority and one in which they are still barred by the Anglican and Roman Catholic Churches. The Congregational Church has had women ministers, who are equal in every way with men, since 1917. Maude Royden (1876–1956) founded the Society for the Ministry of Women in 1929, a movement which aimed to get women ordained as Anglican priests. Yet today, seventy-three years after the start of the movement, the issue of women as priests remains a controversial one. Deaconesses are the only order for women in the Anglican Church. The title is the female equivalent to a deacon but without leading to the priesthood. Deaconesses can, at the discretion of the bishop, assist at the communion service, baptize in the absence of a priest, bury the dead and read marriage banns at morning and evening prayers. They cannot administer the Holy Sacrament. They are ordained women 'set apart for special service in the Christian church.' In the Anglican Church the system by which priests are appointed to a church is governed by a hierarchy or synod. Some parishioners would object if a woman priest was 'forced upon them'. In the Congregational Church ministers are 'called', which means that their appointment is by mutual consent of the applicant and the congregation. A woman can't be appointed against the wishes of the people of the church. Elsie always wanted to be judged as a minister and preacher and not as a woman. Elsie also felt that prejudice often came from women members: 'They are most violently opposed to the pulpit being permanently occupied by one of their own sex.'

At home John and Elsie would often argue about ordination. John would just occasionally ruffle Elsie's feathers by saying, 'You are not properly ordained. You can only be ordained with "the laying on of hands".' Such banter was never serious since both firmly believed in the other's vocation! John felt that 'it was high time the

73

Anglican Church allowed women the ultimate priesthood.'

Elsie was the only woman delegate selected to lead one of the official services of worship at the second Assembly of the World Council of Churches, held in Evanston, Illinois in the USA. For this Elsie had to prepare her speech several months in advance so that it could be translated into French and German. At the Assembly, Elsie said she was glad for all women that they asked her to take part in leading worship at the Assembly. 'I feel keenly,' she said, 'that women should learn to discuss things and think, rather than just feel.' She crossed the Atlantic to the USA in one of Cunard's liners – an entry among the guests list records 'Rev L. C. Chamberlain'!

If Elsie was the first lady chaplain, she was also the first woman to hold a major position in any denomination. She was the only woman minister on the staff of Religious Broadcasting. 'I've never set out to be this or that,' she said. 'I've tackled each job as it came along. I am an ordained minister who just happens to be a woman!' She was regarded as a novelty by many who first heard her preach. But throughout her ministry, Elsie never sought any special consideration on account of her sex. 'God has made us all different, with a contribution to make, dependent not on sex but on the degree of dedication.' She was quite adamant that there were neither theological nor doctrinal grounds for the exclusion of women from the full Christian ministry. Women have always played a great role in church history as saints, martyrs, organizers and spiritual guides. St Paul said, 'There is neither male nor female in Jesus Christ.' Elsie expressed her feelings on this by writing. 'Sex is not really important but I want obstacles removed from the way of people who want to follow what they feel God is telling them to do.'

On page 75 is an interesting letter from Elsie, published in *The Citizen* in 1969, regarding the ordination of women.

Throughout her life Elsie was a staunch advocate for the rights of women. She felt women should have equal rights to men and sat on many committees to emphasize her

74

Does the priestly function really depend on sex?

SIR — IN 25 YEARS MINISTRY I'VE HEARD SOME HILARIOUS REASONS WHY WOMEN SHOULD NOT BE ORDAINED BUT DID THE BISHOP OF GLOUCESTER IN THE INTERVIEW IN THE CITIZEN REALLY SAY, "YOU CAN'T IMAGINE A BISHOP IN A SKIRT."

Does the man in the street imagine him in anything else? What does he think a cassock looks like to a mere man, or woman for that matter?

If the Bishop thinks that lack of trousers is the only impediment to the ordination of women in the Church of England, I'm sure that can easily be rectified; though our Lord and His Apostles did not find them necessary.

Seriously, are we not belittling the sacred Ministry by suggesting that God's call to service relates to the type of clothes a person wears. Or for that matter, in this sex-ridden age, is it not a pity to suggest that the priestly function depends on sex I find that it does not.

REV. ELSIE
CHAMBERLAIN.
The City Temple,
Holborn Viaduct,
London.

support for the expression of the female point of view.

In 1962 Elsie was selected to preach at the central service of the Women's World Day of Prayer in the presence of Her Majesty The Queen Mother. In the seventies she was vice-president of the Six Point Group, a non-political body founded in 1921 and dedicated to furthering the equality of women. From 1984–1985 she was the national president of the Free Church Women's Council.

8

Conregational Minister

After her marriage to John Elsie could not relinquish her vocation. She and John were in mutual agreement that it should continue. Elsie received a letter which stated that there was a vacancy for a pastor at the Vineyard Congregational Church in Richmond, Surrey – about six miles from Hampton. The letter went on to say that there was a question as to whether that church was 'modern' enough for a woman to be considered for the pastorate. Elsie wrote immediately, 'Please don't tell them that I'm a woman, let me go and preach there as a supply – they will then judge me as a preacher and not my sex!'

Arrangements were made for Elsie to be a visiting preacher. The church members took to her. She was an excellent preacher; she had charisma and a caring personality. She was invited to become their pastor. The appointment was offered on a temporary basis because of her health problems. Elsie wrote, 'I saw my doctor at the beginning of the week and he was not very cheering. He says the winter will probably be decisive as to my future health. If I undertake work that prevents my resting when tired or takes me into the cold and wet, the incurable form of arthritis may replace the variety from which I have been suffering. I neither want to become an invalid nor saddle your church with one. Therefore, it seems wise to come to a six months arrangement and if I am still on my feet by the end of March, I think the worst will be over and we can talk about things again.'

Elsie was inducted to the ministry of Vineyard Congregational Church on Friday, 14 November 1947. This ministry was to last seven years, mostly on a part-time basis. John, who was present at the induction service, was asked to say a few words. His remarks caused some hilarity: 'I assure you not only of my wife's unerring ability to keep the Church of England in order but also the fact that that ability will be passed on to the Vineyard in more than one way! I know very well that she is first rate in everything – otherwise I would not have married her.'

The principal chaplain in the RAF was unable to attend but he sent this message in a letter, dated 31 October 1947, to the church secretary: 'We know the good work that your new Minister is capable of and we are sure that under her ministry your Church will go forward . . . '

Elsie did work diligently and the church did go forward! According to one member, 'She is one of the best preachers the church has had for some time.' She started to tutor a group of children learning to play the violin (I was one of that group). At the same time you must bear in mind that she had another group playing at John's church. She conducted the large oratorios at Christmas and Easter – it was often a different one from that being performed in Hampton! She also visited the sick and took an active part in church organisations and meetings.

She left the Vineyard when she took up her full-time appointment with the BBC and she did not have a church between 1955–1968. She was much sought after as a visiting preacher in Congregational churches in the British Isles. In the fifties and sixties John and I saw very little of Elsie. She was often away; her vocation in the ministry was the most important thing to her. She used to say, 'Thank God I have a long suffering husband and daughter!'

In May 1955 Elsie hit the headlines again. She was voted chairman elect of the Congregational Union of England and Wales. This was the first time such a position had been given to a woman. Here is the letter from the Rev Leslie Cooke, dated 12 May 1955, informing Elsie of this great honour.

77

THE CONGREGATIONAL UNION
OF ENGLAND & WALES

Secretary: The Rev. LESLIE E. COOKE, B.A.,D.D.
Finance: Mr. HAROLD SIMPSON, A.S.A.A.   CENTRAL 3936
Publications: Mr. BERNARD HONESS CENTRAL 1954 AND 4470
TELEGRAMS: MEMORIAL, CENT, LONDON

MEMORIAL HALL
FARRINGDON STREET
LONDON, E.C.4

12th May 1955

PRIVATE AND CONFIDENTIAL

My dear Elsie,

      I have received from the solicitors to-day the announcement of your election to the Chair of the Congregational Union of England and Wales for the year 1956-57.

      I am sure that this announcement will give great satisfaction to the Assembly and the denomination as a whole. It is a recognition of the distinctive service that you have given through the years. and of course you will hold the historic position as being the first woman ever to be elected to the Chair of the Union. I am only sorry that I shall not be in the Secretarial Chair to work with you, but I would like to say personally how great a satisfaction this result has given to me.

      Now I must enjoin you strictly to keep this information completely and utterly to yourself. It must be disclosed to no one until the announcement is made on Monday evening, and I know that I can respect your confidence in this matter.

      You will, of course, be expected briefly to respond to the announcement when it is made on Monday.

            With love,

                Yours,

The Rev.Elsie Chamberlain, B.D.

Before agreeing to stand for the chairmanship Elsie made sure that her friend and mentor, the Rev Muriel Paulden, was not a candidate; she would not have stood against her. Congratulations poured in from everywhere. I reproduce one from a Roman Catholic priest:

78

15/1/[57] FROM THE REVD. DR. GORDON ALBION. SUTTON PARK. GUILDFORD. (TEL.4630)

My dear Elsie,

Sincere congratulations on your promotion. Suppose in Popish terminology you are a Right Reverend MONSIGNORA. With people like yourself at the top, remain is that much nearer — at anyrate, union [...] if not of [...] fact.

Blessings on your work,

[signature]

She took up her appointment in May 1956 and it lasted for one year. She did not use her high office for propaganda for the ministry of women. 'I believe that a minister is a minister regardless of whether that person is a he or a she. And it is as a minister that I shall be serving the Union,' she said. She was the Union's chief spokesman for the year. As the Congregational 'Archbishop', she didn't have special embroidered robes or stole. She wore a plain black suit and white blouse under an academic gown and her striking Bachelor of Divinity hood of maroon and black, underlined in white. Elsie found delivering the inaugural speech as chairman, at the start of her year, to be an awesome task. The presidental address was entitled, 'White to Harvest'. She spoke clearly, simply and very forcibly and in a way that all might understand. She acquitted herself with strength and humour and was more than adequate for the far from easy task of guiding such a large gathering. Elsie then spent her year preaching in as many Congregational churches as she could and she chaired many meetings. As the representative head of the Congregational Church, there were other honours. She was invited to a Buckingham

Palace garden party; she represented the Union at the Remembrance Sunday ceremony at the Cenotaph. The year 1956 to 1957 was a very happy and memorable one for Elsie, and she loved it – even though she made quite a few night trips on trains!

'First woman chairman of the Union, first woman RAF chaplain, first ordained woman on the staff of the BBC, first Congregational minister to be a vicar's wife. With all these first-class accomplishments we must expect a first-class year of chairmanship in which we know we will will not be disappointed', *Christian World* May 1955. And we weren't.

After her year as chairman, Elsie continued to preach in churches throughout the British Isles whilst at the same time continuing her 'missionary' work with the BBC. She also worked as a vicar's wife, supporting John and his parishioners whenever possible.

After Elsie retired from the BBC in 1967 she tried her hand at lecturing and teaching – an experience which she didn't enjoy. She was a preacher rather than a teacher, so she returned to her calling as a minister. She was unanimously appointed by the members of the City Temple, Holborn Viaduct, London, to be an associate minister in 1968. She worked in partnership with the Rev Kenneth Slack. The City Temple is regarded by some as having the status of a 'Cathedral for Non-conformists.' Elsie was anxious to exploit the locality of this church. She was intent on building up the 'outgoing church'. The church should be in use seven days a week and not just on Sundays. Her eventual aim was to form an 'interdenominational youth discussion council.' Lunch-time services were arranged – the church was opened to all regardless of their race and denomination.

She did not remain long at the City Temple. John's health was beginning to deteriorate and she wished to be nearer to him. She accepted a part-time appointment at Hutton Free Church, on the outskirts of Brentwood in Essex. This was much nearer to Greensted and Elsie was able to spend more time with her ailing husband.

While she was minister at Hutton Free Church Elsie continued to stress what she saw as a failure by the church to recognize a need for God among those outside it. She formed another orchestra and introduced a Monday Washing Day Coffee Club for local women – any lady was welcome to join regardless of her creed and race. To Elsie, 'a half empty church was a half full church!' She worked to achieve a full church. On one occasion Elsie played a trick on the members of Hutton Free Church. They held a 'Tramps' Supper'. Elsie came in for a quick chat and then disappeared. Later that same evening a very scruffy old dirty tramp arrived for a free dinner! The members were quite shocked. But hidden beneath the layers of dirt was Elsie, having a 'bit of fun'!

John suffered a massive heart attack in January 1978. He was rushed to Epping Hospital where he went into a coma and was placed on a life support machine. I was summoned to the hospital. John and I had always been close. When I arrived he opened his eyes very briefly and smiled at me and then went back into a coma, never to wake up again. He died in the early hours of Sunday, 28 January 1978. I had always considered myself as John's child and I loved and adored him dearly. Elsie had lost her husband, and for the first time in her life she turned to me for support and comfort. It was John's death that made me realize that Elsie was very fond of me and she began to show it. She had a respect for me and my husband that did not exist in John's lifetime. John's funeral service took place in his beloved Greensted Church. The local clergy, in all their robes, were the choir and the Bishop of Chelmsford, John Trillo, who had been a fellow student at Kings' College, gave the address. The little church was filled with friends and parishioners to pay their last respects to dear, loving John. His ashes were placed in the Garden of Remembrance at Greensted Church.

After John's death Elsie had to move from the rectory. Many of the personal effects, collected over the years, were sold, including John's wonderful library – for the whole of which we were offered a paltry £100! Elsie moved into the manse at Hutton, which was a much smaller house than the grand, spacious rectory, which she loved. Elsie was lonely and perplexed. She had relied on John so much. He was able to tell her to 'Take it easy, girl' – which no one else dared to say! He was her soulmate, somebody with whom she could discuss, meditate, laugh and relax. Elsie was energetic to a fault but John could calm her down, recharge her batteries and give encouragement. John's ending prayer at nighttime was 'Please God, help Elsie to sleep.' Their marriage had lasted thirty-one years and was founded on mutual love and respect. Each had understanding for the other and each gave service, with fervour and devotion, to their churches. Elsie used to say, 'I look forward to meeting my husband again but that doesn't make it any the less lonely for me now.'

9

Congregational Federation

Elsie could have retired after John's death but she felt her work was not yet complete. She continued with renewed stamina and vigour and she spent the rest of her life helping to build up the Congregatioal Federation and its centre in Nottingham. In 1972, before John's death, the question of unity came to the fore. The Rev Kenneth Slack, Elsie's ministerial partner at the City Temple, was in favour of the union between the Congregational and Presbyterian Churches. This union was to become the United Reformed Church (URC). Elsie did not support the union because she felt it was not what the majority of Congregationalists desired. Overleaf is a letter from Elsie to the Rev Kenneth Slack which appeared in *Christian World* on 17 February 1972.

Elsie continued her ministry at Hutton while making herself available to preach in Congregational churches which were without a minister. She was also taking an active part in forming the Federation. It was about this time I noticed that Elsie was beginning to age. Her lovely dark brown hair had turned grey and she seemed to have adopted a uniform, wearing a full length black cassock and a forked clerical collar. When she was seventy Elsie moved to the West Country to take up the ministries of North Street Church in Taunton and the Congregational Church in Chulmleigh, North Devon. She spent Thursday to Sunday morning in Taunton and from Sunday evening to Wednesday in Chulmleigh. She drove from church to church, a distance of nearly forty miles, and had two

An open letter from Elsie Chamberlain to Kenneth Slack

'The Judgement of Gamaliel still holds.
If this thing is of God, it will stand—whether it is United
Reformed Church or Congregational Federation or both or neither'

DEAR KEN, Unaccustomed as I am to having my letters published (they are always more "utility" than "belles") you started this, so don't blame me!

It was nice of you to offer me a way in if I changed my mind.. May I reciprocate if you were to wish to continue in the essential freedoms of Congregationalism.

You will have noted, Ken, that I waited till everyone had had a chance to vote; not because I think I rock any boats, but so that no one could say I had.

But when, after a "free" vote I found pressure was being brought to bear on the "noes", then I felt I must stand with those whose consciences held them where they had belonged for so long in the kind of churchmanship that, as well as being New Testament in origin, seems qualified by its nature to be a kind of catalytic agent among the churches.

Ah well. Which way went the Spirit from me to thee is an old question—and which spirit any way? Neither can I say, nor I imagine would, you, "This is God's will" of either way, without the prefix "I hope" or "I believe" or "I think". Those who do, make me doubt and challenge, not "the establishment", but the authority of the speaker.

What I do not doubt is that Christ prayed for the unity of his disciples and therefore that he believed it possible that they should be united. But I do not think he was praying for organic or constitutional unity, but for a unity of spirit that would be of the same essential unity that he shared with the Father. Uniformity was not a thing he seemed to aim at or expect.

I don't mind what sub-title any Christian has. I'm happy to receive Communion with him, or from him, and to reciprocate. I'm happy to be blessed by him—or her, of course!—and to worship God in other forms and according to other rites; but to be allowed also that freedom of order which can help people in their search for God, according to their differing needs. And for this, one needs not to be a URC first.

Of course I have never believed that unity would come about by us all becoming Independents! How could I, with an Anglican father and a higher Anglican husband!

And if Independence means to some, doing what they like, they are not among the continuing congregationalists I gathered with recently. And I'm sure you could guess, Ken, that if that's all it is to me, I would have left its ranks years ago.

I believe that my husband's churchmanship and mine are part of the CHURCH—though so different. In the Church of Jesus Christ I believe there must be room for all the given insights of all forms of churchmanship.

That is why this steamrollering together of two forms of churchmanship, each with very different insights, does not seem to be a step towards unity. Some things of value are bound to go down the drain.

I'm always telling people that we must learn to disagree without being disagreeable: necessary since one correspondent already would have had me crack my skull when I came "off the fence" on the other side from him. You can see how easily people come to cutting off ears—or heads—over religious questions when emotions have been so overworked. Let's not come to this.

The judgement of Gamaliel still holds. If this thing is of God, it will stand—whether it is URC or Congregational Federation or both or neither. And I shall go on working and praying for the unity of Christ's Church in the immediate company of people willing to face the consequences of following their consciences and in the wider company of friendships across all the denominational barriers.

The Spirit, like the wind, still blows where it pleases. Ordinary people must be free to breathe it—freer I think, than the tight lacing of the constitutional corset of URC allows.

Sincerely,

ELSIE

manses to look after! In 1983 she ceased to be the minister at Chulmleigh. She was succeeded by the Rev Elaine Marsh, who she had met in America. She remained at Taunton. Her church was in the heart of the busy shopping area. She used its prime locality to try to woo the non-church goer. She set herself the task of introducing religion by stressing how it could enrich one's life. She started classes for people of any denomination, Christian or even atheist, to study the Bible and learn how to talk about their faith and beliefs more easily. Among those who attended these classes were many shoppers, some of whom came out of curiosity, while others were keen to participate.

It was not long before Elsie had two jobs again! She was offered an honorary pastorate at the Federation Centre Church in Nottingham. She accepted the post and for the next two and a half years she preached in Nottingham for the morning service and at Taunton for the evening one. She drove down the motorways after the morning service and was never late for the evening one! Her age and sex was no handicap in running two churches simultaneously. She combined this dual ministry until she was seventy seven, by which time her health was deteriorating. She was diagnosed as having a non-maligant lymphona which required a radium implant, but she continued to work even though she was so ill.

Between 1973–75 Elsie was the second president of the Congregational Federation, Lady Stansgate being the first. She represented the Federation at the International Congregational Fellowship, held in America in 1981. She was the Federation's spokesperson for ecumenical affairs. It was here that Elsie predicted that future generations would regard the endless committees and discussions on church unity as 'a joke and wasted years'. She would say 'There is only one God – it is man, in his communication with God, that is different. Differences stimulate our thinking and we should disagree or agree without being dogmatic or unpleasant. It is up to the churches to recognize individual differences and requirements and not stifle these with hierarchy and dogma.'

Why did Elsie support the splinter group of Congregationalists from the URC? She was such an advocate of church unity that many people have found her actions inexplicable. She had attended two World Council of Churches assemblies, the first held in Amsterdam in 1948. John and Elsie both attended – John as a reporter for a Christian newspaper and Elsie as a 'visiting participant'. Elsie wrote: 'It was one of the times, we were aware of the power of the Spirit propelling that great mixed company which had gathered.' Elsie was also a member of the British Council of Churches, which comprise the major denominations, apart from the Roman Catholic Church. She wrote, 'Keen as we were doing things together, we did not believe that unity meant uniformity; nor could we believe in the idea of one great church.' It was, therefore, ironic that it was the amalgamation between the Congregational and Presbyterian Churches, which formed the URC in 1972, that caused Elsie more distress than anything else in her career.

Elsie consulted with other Congregationalists, including Lady Stansgate, and they opposed the move. Both Lady Stansgate and Elsie were staunch believers in church unity. They felt that the great moral issues of our time, especially poverty in the midst of plenty and the threat of nuclear war, pose questions that could not be answered in spiritual isolation. But Lady Stansgate was concerned about the dangers to Congregationalism if it joined the URC and she warned Elsie. This led to a study of the documents in greater detail. They decided to come out of the URC plan because they thought it would mean Congregationalists giving away the things most important to them.

The Declaration of Faith and Order is a long carefully worded document, which states: 'Congregationalism is that form of Church polity which rests on the independence and autonomy of each local church.'

The Congregation Union is not a legislative authority but serves to advise, encourage and help the churches and to express their common mind. The URC is a legislative

87

authority. All members of the Congregational Church, being Christians, are 'priests unto God'. Each church is dependent and responsible for itself and the business is conducted collectively by all its members. The responsibility of a Congregationalist is to provide what the Holy Spirit wants in that church. The Congregational Church has no superior authorities. The URC has a synod and synods are authoritative. People should not be tied down and told what to do. This is also why Elsie could not aspire to become a Church of England priest. She wanted to be governed by the people of the church and not by a synod! Elsie was sure that every church would be in a stronger position to serve the community, as a whole, if it was united. What each denomination believes is fundamentally the same. It is the way it is expressed that is different. It is the duty of individual Christian to establish communion with God. Everybody should be able to worship in his, or her, own way; if incense is wanted, it should be available. She wanted a broader base for unity but not uniformity – 'unity in diversity'.

As a teenager, I had the privilege to attend an ecumenical service in St Peter's Cathedral in Geneva, Switzerland. Here there were many Christians of different denominations and races worshipping God in the same building. *Now thank we all Our God* was one of the hymns and people sang it together in the words of their own language. At prayer time those who wished to kneel, knelt; those who wished to sit, sat and so on. The service was taken in three languages, English, French and German. We were all part of that service and each of us expressed our faith in our own way and language. I have never forgotten that wonderful experience. Unity between the churches was a subject very close to Elsie's heart.

After the union of the United Reformed Churches, there were about three hundred churches which remained outside as independent, to form the Congregational Federation. The Congregational Centre at Castle Gate in Nottingham is the headquarters for all Congregationalists in the British

Isles who resisted amalgamation with the Presbyterian Church. The Federation bought back from the URC the old Castle Gate Congregational Church. This building dates from 1864 and it stands on the site where a group of Congregationalists first worshipped in the mid-seventeenth century. It was a huge, lofty, cold building and in a terrible state of dereliction. With the aid of grants and members of the city community task force, financed by the Manpower Services Commission, this church was converted into a complex. A floor was put in at gallery level. The church and organ remained above the new flooring. The ground floor was converted into offices, a cafeteria, a bookshop and reading room. The rambling Sunday School building, which adjoins the church, was donated to the Federation. Now known as Cleaves Hall, this was transformed into a forty-bedroomed conference centre with showers and toilets, kitchens, lecture rooms, concert hall, roof garden and three self-contained flats. Cleaves Hall is used as a students' hostel during term-time and as a conference centre during the vacations. Ramps and lifts were installed so that the handicapped could benefit from the amenities on offer at the site.

When Elsie finally moved to Nottingham, she and her brother, Ronald bought one of the self-contained flats as a memorial to their mother. It is known as the Annie Chamberlain flat and Elsie was its first tenant. Elsie took upon herself the duties of an unpaid warden of the hostel. As a minister of the church she continued her pastorate work, which included caring for drug addicts, alcoholics and the homeless. Sometimes she placed her own life in danger whilst dealing with these people. One alcoholic became so violent when Elsie took away his full bottle of wine that he threatened to stab her. Elsie, in her calm and authoritative voice, managed to persuade the offending man that he was not a murderer!

In 1990 Elsie celebrated her eightieth birthday and her fiftieth year in the ministry. I phoned some of her friends in Nottingham to draw this to their attention. They held a special presentation ceremony for her. Elsie never retired, she just kept going, drawing on what seemed to be boundless energy. But at the beginning of 1991 Elsie was taken into hospital. She made a temporary recovery and was discharged in the care of Henry and Paddy Morris, who live within easy reach of the hospital and Nottingham. She spent her last week in their home and lovely garden. Elsie loved the springtime and the weather was just perfect. She was then re-admitted into hospital, where she went into a deep sleep.

I was summoned to the hospital and although Elsie never opened her eyes she knew I was there. She somehow managed to turn herself to face me – she became totally relaxed and was at peace. She died in the evening of 10 April 1991 at the age of eighty-one.

As a teenager and young mother I had resented having to share Elsie with others, I respected and was in awe of her, but by golly, I do miss my mum! We all loved her and she has left a gap in our lives. I am proud to be the adopted daughter of John and Elsie Garrington.

Elsie's funeral service was held in her last church, the Congregational Centre Church in Nottingham. It was attended by more than 400 friends and colleagues. She was cremated and her ashes were placed beside John's in Greensted's Garden of Remembrance.

Elsie's life was affected by many factors. She had been influenced by her mother, who had a very domineering personality. Religion played a large part in the family home, where the church and its work was a major point of discussion. Her parents and teachers encouraged her to work hard in order to achieve her full potential. She always set herself high standards. Music and drawing were two pastimes at which she excelled and the love for these remained with her all her life.

Elsie's wartime experiences gave her the opportunity to mix with people from a much wider range of backgrounds than she experienced in her formative years. She learnt to work very hard. The church became a place of refuge where calm and peace was sought by people under emotional stress. The church was a working unit, not only catering for spiritual needs, but also for the material needs of the population. She became a life-long advocate for peace and supported 'Amnesty International', an organization which works to assist those imprisoned for their beliefs and ideals. It opposes unfair trials and torture, cruelty, degrading treatment and the imposing of the death penalty.

Elsie tried to make the distinction between achievement in an ideal world and what could be expected in real life. Circumstances made it impractical to insist on the rigid morals standards in which she had been brought up. She strove to improve the quality of people's lives and at the same time to increase their faith, rather than to condemn them for their misdemeanours and shortcomings.

A memorial service was planned to include representation of many facets of her life and achievements. It took place at the City Temple, Holborn Viaduct, London. Many people were surprised by the choice of that church. All I can say is that I felt sure this was Elsie's wish. The Rev Edwin Robertson, a former BBC colleague and lifelong friend, gave the address. Mr Tony Benn MP, a son of Lord and Lady Stansgate, contributed an account of the RAF chaplaincy issue. The Rev Jackie Petrie RAF led prayers – Jackie was the next woman to be appointed a chaplain in the RAF after Elsie. The Rev E. Rhea, present head of Religious Broadcasting, BBC, also led prayers. Her old school, Channing School for Girls, provided a beautiful choir and her friend, Miss Trixie Norcott, played the organ. Her nephew, Geoffrey and the eldest grandchild of Annie and Jim Chamberlain, read from the Jerusalem Bible (Elsie had been general editor of Mowbray's new series of mini commentaries on the Jerusalem Bible). Three Congregational ministers also participated – Rev Dr Janet Wootton, who conducted the service; Rev Irene Blaney, a personal friend and a male pastor, Rev Leslie Morrison, who gave the blessing. The ladies of her former church, Hutton Free Church, Brentwood, served the refreshments and members

91

of the new Islington Chapel, acted as ushers.

I received many letters of sympathy. The Rt Hon Sir Edward du Cann, former MP for Taunton, wrote, 'I greatly admired her for what she did and what she was.' Miss Helen Thomas, a carer for the British Legion, wrote, 'I am sure you must miss Elsie a lot but she had a full and satisfying life of which you were a very important part.' However the message from the present Archbishop of Canterbury – 'Wasn't she a marvellous person?' must have John and Elsie chuckling in Heaven!

This book, Rev Elsie Chamberlain, Mrs Garrington and Mum, is your life. Traditional barriers meant so little to you and you surmounted so many of them. What a life it was, devoted to furthering your beliefs and ideals! Your work and achievements will be remembered long after your death. Your work will inspire others for years – maybe for centuries – to come.

ACKNOWLEDGEMENTS

Grateful acknowledgement is given to the following for permission to reproduce photographs and media extracts:

The *BBC* (Cover photograph Copyright A 43358); *West Essex Gazette*; Messers Langfier; Photographic Agencies Ltd.; Elliot & Fry Ltd.; Planet News Ltd.; Keystone Press Agency Ltd.; Ivor Ashmore; James Jarche (*Picture Goer*); Walter Stoneman, J. Russell & Sons; Central Press Photos, Ltd.; Publiphoto Ltd.; Roy Cook; Adelaide *Advertiser*; *Woman and Home*; *Daily Sketch*.

The Author and publishers wish to express their thanks to:

Mr Tony Benn MP for permission to publish the letter from Archbishop Fisher to his late father, Lord Stansgate; Mrs F Chamberlain for permission to publish Geoffrey de Freitas' letter to her late husband Ronald Chamberlain; the *BBC* for permission to quote 'Epitaph'.

The author's thanks also goes to:

Mrs Florence Chamberlain, who gave invaluable help on early family history.
Dr Leonard Williams for his time, patience and advice.
Mr Colin Williams for photocopying.